THE
CRIMEWA
GUIDE TO
HOME
SECURITY

Sue Cook

BBC Books

Picture credits:
ASTRAL ACCESSORIES (MIDLANDS) LTD
page 65; BANHAM PATENT LOCKS (photo,
Aardvark) page 21; BARNABY'S PICTURE
LIBRARY front cover (Neighbourhood
Watch), pages 48 and 119; BRITISH
TELECOM page 104; BURGESS TOOLS LTD
page 37; CEKA WORKS LTD (photo, Tony
Timmington) page 82; CHUBB LOCK CO.
front cover (window lock), pages 9
(bottom left), 11 (top), 13, 32 and 33;
HOME OFFICE page 53; METRO PRODUCTS
LTD page 76; MODERN VITALCALL page
51; TOPLINE INTERNATIONAL page 101
(Walk Easy aerosol alarm); T. TURNER
LTD front cover (gear lock) and page 67.
    The remaining photographs were
taken for the BBC

Text credits:
The quotations in sections 1 and 2 are
reproduced with permission from *Your
Security*, published by Security
Publications Ltd. The chart on pages
58–9 was supplied by General Accident
and the information on page 46 by Sun
Alliance.

All information and prices were correct
on going to press.

Illustrations: Brian Robins

Published by BBC Books
a division of BBC Enterprises Ltd
Woodlands
80 Wood Lane
London W12 0TT

First published 1988
© Sue Cook 1988
ISBN 0 563 20655 1

Typeset in 11/13 Univers
Printed and bound in Great Britain by
Redwood Burn Ltd, Trowbridge, Wiltshire

Contents

Introduction

Acknowledgements

As I explain in the Introduction, this book draws together practical information on security from many different sources and I would like to thank the following for their help: Association of British Insurers, British Telecom, Consumers' Association, General Accident, Metropolitan Police Crime Prevention Services, Home Office Crime Prevention Centre, Kidscape, London Rape Crisis Centre, Modern Alarms, Polycell, Security Publications Ltd, Sun Alliance.

If you want a book that gives you DIY advice on fitting locks etc. then I would recommend Jack Hay and Ian Penberthy's book *Do Your Own Home Security* (Foulsham Press, 1985). In a higher price bracket, *The Personal Security Handbook*, published by Sphere (1987), is an extremely comprehensive guide to all aspects of safety. The London Cycling Campaign publish an excellent booklet called *On Your Bike* which gives advice on bicycle maintenance and road safety as well as how to protect your bike from theft. There are many books on the market now about personal safety, especially for women. Diana Lamplugh's *Beating Aggression* (Weidenfeld, 1988) is an especially thoughtful and useful book. For children I would particularly recommend the video called *Strong Kids, Safe Kids* published by CIC Video and the Kidscape leaflet mentioned on page 117.

Finally I would like to thank Judith Lowe, Michelle Elliot and Helen Kenward for the advice and information they gave me when writing the section on personal and child safety. And last, but definitely not least, many thanks to Inspector Greg Lawrence of the Home Office Crime Prevention Centre who has been our patient and enthusiastic consultant.

Sue Cook
June 1988

Introduction

All that is necessary for evil to triumph is for good men to do nothing.

Edmund Burke (1729–97)

On *Crimewatch* we usually deal with the more serious crimes – those that the police are most anxious to solve quickly because the criminals involved may be dangerous and are likely to strike again. However, as we point out each month, these crimes are relatively rare. By far the most common ones are the everyday thefts and burglaries that take up most of a police officer's time. These are crimes involving private homes and cars, or 'muggings' where handbags, wallets or any other possessions are snatched from people in the street.

Government figures show that there has been a steady increase in the number of burglaries over the past few years. With police resources already overstretched, it makes sense for us, the public, to take more responsibility for protecting ourselves and our property.

The police are increasingly taking on an advisory role in the community, helping to organise people to combat and prevent crime in their own areas. Neighbourhood Watch or Home Watch schemes now work very effectively in many parts of the country. Minding your own business is no longer the best policy if you want to be a good neighbour!

The purpose of this book is to bring together all the advice that is currently published by the police, insurance companies, security firms, alarm manufacturers, DIY groups, and all the other organisations involved in helping to protect our persons, our property or both.

Being burgled is shocking and distressing. No amount of insurance money can compensate for the feeling of violation that a housebreaker leaves behind, nor for the loss of those items which may not be of so much worth financially, but are priceless in terms of sentimental value. So if this book can prevent a burglary happening to you, it will have been well worth writing!

Section 1

Home security

A burglar's delight: 1) open sideway allowing easy access to the back of the house; 2) unchained ladder; 3) open garage doors revealing an empty garage; 4) no-one home to empty the letter box; 5) high hedge providing plenty of cover; 6) small window open; 7) easy-to-force louvre windows; 8) flat roof offering easy access.

If a criminal is absolutely determined to get into your home, he will; but 80 per cent of all burglaries are carried out by the 'casual' or 'opportunist' thief who is likely to live a short distance from your home and is probably a male, aged between 14 and 17. Most people are amazed to learn that the average age of a housebreaker is just 15 years old. The tragedy is that of this 80 per cent, most burglaries could be prevented if householders took a few simple, inexpensive precautions. We often inadvertently invite crime. In a quarter of all burglaries, the burglars get in through insecure windows and doors. People have simply forgotten to close or lock them! Never assume that it won't happen to you. Everybody has something worth stealing. Think about it!

Obviously most of us do not want to live in a kind of Fort Knox – nor do we need to. What is important is to be sure that the locks we fit on our outside doors and windows are adequate, and that we remember to use them. It is true that good strong locks are not cheap and usually need to be installed by a locksmith, but they are definitely worth the expense.

❝ . . . people are really stupid when it comes to protecting the back of the house. Out of sight, out of mind is the order of the day. People go out and leave the windows open, doors unlocked, and even doors open! ❞

Doors

Front door

You could use a five-lever mortise lock or a rim automatic deadlock on your front door. But an ordinary rim lock is easy for a burglar to overcome.

Five-lever mortise lock

This type of lock is stronger and more secure than a rim lock but only fit it yourself if you really know what you are doing. You should also have a welded striking box. A flat striking plate is less secure because it can be levered off with a sharp instrument.

Rim automatic deadlock

If your door is hollow or too thin to install a mortise lock, fit the best-quality rim deadlock, using *long, strong* screws. A door which is deadlocked is much more difficult to force open. Also, with a deadlock, the door cannot be opened without the key, so a burglar cannot use the front door to get out of the house with bulky items.

If you buy a lock which conforms to British Standards (BS 3621) you can be sure the quality will be good. Look for the kite mark.

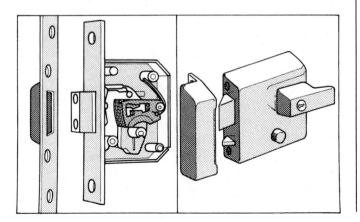

LEFT: a five-lever mortise lock and welded striking plate.
RIGHT: a rim deadlock. This one can be locked from the inside with a key (semi-automatic).

9

Once I'd loaded up my case with all the lucrative bits and pieces I would leave by the front door. Let's face it, it's perfectly natural to see someone leaving with a case or bag in their hand, right? Chances are that the front door had only a rim latch so it was a quick twist and out job. Of course it was a different story if the front door had a deadlock. . . I couldn't open this easily from the inside or outside . . . and you can't turn it by putting your hand through the letter box, or through a broken glass panel in the door.

Back door

The best lock to use on your back door, or on an interconnecting door between the garage and the house, is a five-lever mortise sashlock (see illustration opposite) because it combines a lock and handle.

Patio doors

Patio doors are particularly vulnerable to burglars because they can be prised and lifted out. Bear in mind that a man wielding a jemmy can exert 1 ton of pressure, and a man with a stout shovel can exert infinitely more. There are patio door locks available (see illustration opposite) which consist of a key-operated, surface-mounted bolt on one door which shoots into a mortise on the other door. Fit one of these top and bottom. There is just one proviso: check with your double glazing contractor before fitting to make sure you are using locks that are suitable and that you are not invalidating any existing guarantees.

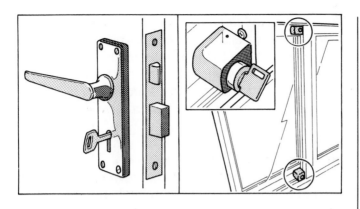

LEFT: a five-lever mortise sashlock (ie with a handle). RIGHT: key-operated patio window locks.

Outward-opening doors with hinges on the outside

Doors with hinges on the outside can be forced or lifted quite easily, so you should fit one hinge bolt below the top hinge and another above the bottom hinge. Hinge bolts (also known as dog-bolts) are solid metal cylinders which fit into holes on the frame when the door is closed.

On double doors, such as French windows, you will need two mortise security bolts fitted *vertically* top and bottom on the non-opening door. A cheaper alternative to these would be two flush bolts. If your doors have a poor-quality, two-lever sashlock, you will need two more mortise security bolts *horizontally* on the door, also top and bottom.

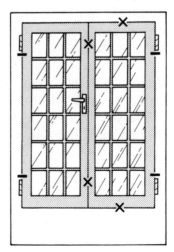

French windows with four hinge bolts (▬) and four mortise security bolts (✗) for really good protection against intruders.

11

"Quite frankly, the majority of locks and bolts that are fitted by builders are cheap and nasty and I could get round them without trying too hard. But if the owner has a decent mortise lock plus key-operated bolts top and bottom, and he's remembered to use 'em, I'm on my bike."

Reinforcing external doors

If your outside doors have flimsy lower panels, these are not only easy to break in through, but can also be used to push the larger items out – the television set, for example. Reinforce the panels with one or two stronger, thicker panels of wood, using screws which are long and strong enough to hold the panels firmly. The screws should be counter-sunk (i.e. flush with the surface) and fitted at intervals of between 6 to 8 inches all round.

Internal doors

Keep internal doors closed but not locked while you are away. Once inside your house, the burglar has more time to work and can afford to make more noise, so you will only end up with smashed doors and further damage. The same applies to locking cupboards and drawers.

When you are on the premises, however, you would obviously have more time to dial 999 if an intruder had to smash down internal doors in order to get to you – as long as you have a phone with you! (But do think about your means of escape in case of fire.)

Windows

Window locks are not designed to stop the determined burglar getting in with a jemmy, but they will deter the casual thief. At least two-thirds of thieves gain entry through windows. Window locks are inexpensive, easy to fit, and should be installed on all downstairs windows and any vulnerable upstairs ones, for example any which overlook a flat extension or garage roof. If, having smashed a hole in the glass, the burglar finds it impossible to open the window by reaching in and releasing the catch, he is unlikely to risk making more noise by smashing the whole pane out – and possibly cutting himself into the bargain!

' *My mates would kill me if they knew I was telling you this, but window locks are a bloomin' nuisance. It just wasn't worth the aggro as far as I was concerned – I'd move on to someone else's house. You see, if I smashed the window I still couldn't open the frame. And to climb in I'd have to break a large part of glass which is dead noisy – and dangerous!* '

Wooden-framed windows

The most secure locks for wooden window frames are those which look like small mortise security bolts.

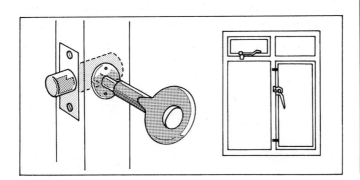

Mortise security bolts suitable for wooden window frames.

Then there are those which fit on to the window handle and prevent it being moved.

One of the kinds of window-handle locks available.

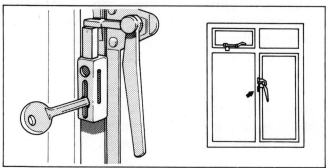

There are also simple locks which you can attach to the window stay.

A window stay lock

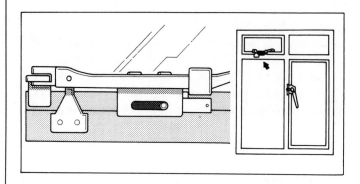

Sash windows

There are cheap and effective bolts available for sash windows. Use two for each frame.

A sash window lock

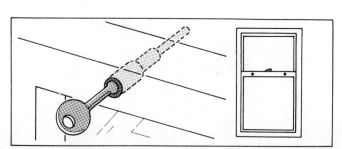

Louvre windows

A burglar can lever louvre windows out of their frames unless they are very firmly glued with epoxy resin. Really, I would recommend that you replace these with more conventional and secure windows, particularly if they are easily accessible to intruders.

Plastic or aluminium-framed windows

You will probably need a specialist from a locksmith or the window supplier to fit extra locks on these. A key-operated locking bolt like that used for patio doors (see page 11) will be needed for sliding windows.

Keys

Burglars do not usually carry keys with them in case they are stopped and searched. It is a criminal offence in itself to be found carrying equipment with the intention of using it for burglary.

The keys to window locks and door bolts should not be left in the locks for obvious reasons, and should be kept in a safe place somewhere out of sight. To be honest, though, hiding keys is usually pointless, as most burglars can find them – so, ideally, no keys should be left indoors at all. Bear in mind that the first action of most burglars once they're in the house is work out which exit they're going to use to escape. If they cannot find any keys they will probably be forced to leave via their entry point, which will limit the amount they are able to steal.

Whatever you do, make sure that everyone in the house knows where the keys are, and has easy access to them in case of fire. When you move into a new house or flat, you should change the locks, just to be on the safe side. You never know how many people might have keys to the front door.

Burglar alarms

One of the most effective deterrents, as far as the opportunist thief is concerned, is the sight of a burglar alarm box on the outside wall of your house. To him, that means trouble. The burglar's two main enemies are time and noise, and a burglar alarm means he'll be fighting both. Usually he'll move on to an easier-looking target.

When I was considering having a burglar alarm installed, I worried at first that it might actually encourage burglars by giving the impression that I had a lot of valuable property in the house. However, I discovered that people living in houses *with* burglar alarms submit far fewer insurance claims than those without. In other words, people who have alarms are burgled less frequently.

To maximise this deterrent effect, make sure the sounder box is clearly visible on the wall. Some people actually go to the trouble of disguising it by painting it the same colour as the house! Make sure that it isn't hidden by any creeper growing up the house and, ideally, there should be a box on the back as well as the front of the house.

If a thief is determined to break in despite the alarm box, and despite having to smash through your locked doors or windows, he will nevertheless know that he has very little time to spend inside the house because someone is likely to respond to the alarm. So he is likely to steal less and do less damage.

In addition to being a deterrent, any burglar alarm should be doing three jobs:

● detecting intruders reliably (and as far as possible ensuring that false alarms do not occur)

● raising the alarm

● enabling you and everyone else in your house or flat to turn the alarm on and off without inadvertently activating it

An amazing 98.6 per cent of alarm calls are false. This represents a lot of wasted police time – not to mention exasperation. In fact, if a particular alarm keeps going off for no reason, then the police (and your neighbours) cease to take it seriously and are likely not to respond to it. So it's important that your alarm system is installed properly, used properly and kept in good working order.

Most alarms feature a delayed exit/entrance circuit which gives you the time to get on or off the premises without setting it off. This time lapse is fixed at between 20 seconds and 2 minutes, and can usually be adjusted to suit you.

The basic system will consist of:

● a control panel or control box – usually installed within easy reach of your usual exit and entry route (for most people, this will be in the hall)

● the detection devices – the various methods available are described on pages 20–3

● the sounder box – the warning bell or siren, and strobe light – fixed to the wall on the outside of the house

Whether you have a siren or a bell, the important thing is that the sound should be urgent enough to attract attention. Most up-to-date systems now have a strobe light attached to the sounder box, as the guidelines laid down in the Control of Pollution Act stipulate that the noise should stop after 20 minutes to save the sanity of your neighbours – especially at night! Once the sound has stopped, the strobe light should keep flashing until someone resets the alarm.

You should opt for a 'self-actuating' sounder. This means that there is a battery inside the sounder box which can take over as power for the bell or siren if a burglar cuts the wires. The battery should be

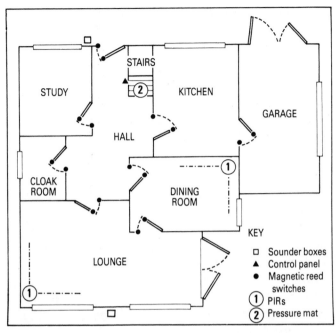

This plan shows possible positions for all the elements of a basic alarm system on the ground floor of a detached house. It would have a separate zone upstairs, and could be augmented by additional detection devices.

checked regularly. Incidentally, many systems also have internal sirens, designed mainly as a psychological disturbance to the burglar who is trying to ignore the alarm as he ransacks the house.

How do burglar alarms work?

Most alarm systems are split up into zones, whereby different areas of the house are controlled by separate circuits which you can opt to include or exclude when you switch the alarm on at the control box. For example, when the family is asleep upstairs, that part of the house can be excluded so that you can make a midnight trip to the bathroom without setting off the alarm, while leaving the downstairs zones switched on.

Each circuit is made up of a series of contacts within the zone. When any of the contacts is broken, the alarm is triggered. A range of devices can be installed on each of these circuits to detect intruders.

Magnetic reed switches

These are contacts which are set into the doors in each zone. When a door is opened the circuit is broken and the alarm is triggered.

Vibration detectors

These are fixed to windows, or their frames and detect vibrations, for example if the glass is broken.

Pressure mats

These are hidden under the carpets at strategic points in the house, in front of certain doors and windows for example, or at the foot of the stairs, or directly in front of any valuables you particularly want to protect. One disadvantage is that after a few months the outline of the mat can start showing through the carpet, warning the intruder to avoid them. If you keep a cat or a dog, pressure mats are not a good idea for obvious reasons!

Heat detectors

A small unit called a PIR (Passive Infra-Red) detector fixed high on the wall in the hall perhaps, or in a main ground floor room, picks up an intruder's body heat and sets off the alarm. It is extremely sensitive and can pick up even the smallest variation above the normal. Again, this is not always a suitable method if you have pets at home, and in any case it is vital for an expert to fix these in exactly the right place to avoid false alarms. They can be set off by bursts of sunshine through a nearby window for example, or by being too near a central heating radiator.

Sound detectors

You can buy free-standing, portable sound sensors which can be placed on the dining room table, for instance, when you go to bed. The sensor then listens for intruders in that one room, and can perhaps

cover a greater range if you leave the internal doors
open. The disadvantage is that these sensors can be triggered by perfectly legitimate noises outside the protected area – in the street perhaps – and so go off by mistake.

There are highly sophisticated alarms available now which can actually respond to the sound of your window being smashed. Windows, especially large ones, always pose a security problem. It is the brief time lapse between the sound of the window being thumped and the tinkle of falling shattered glass that the detector responds to. Some can even tell the difference between a breaking window and a milk bottle breaking!

Ultrasonic detectors
An ultrasonic detector unit, again usually fixed to the wall of a downstairs room, continuously transmits sound waves of such a high frequency that you

A magnetic reed switch (left) and a passive infra-red detector (PIR) (right). Both are types of sensor used in a standard burglar alarm system.

cannot hear them. The waves bounce off the hard surfaces in the room and are picked up again by the same unit. So an intruder entering the room interferes with the frequency of the reflected sound and triggers the alarm.

Radar detectors

This type of detector uses microwaves – very high-frequency radio signals – to sense any movement in the room where it is installed. It is, in effect, a little radar system. Don't worry about the microwaves. They're absolutely harmless – not nearly enough to cook you!

Invisible beam detectors

These are useful outside the house for protecting large areas such as gardens or rooftops. Usually they trigger off security lighting rather than bells or sirens. Often, two invisible parallel beams are installed so that a small creature like a bird or a mouse will not set off the alarm, but an intruder will break both beams and trigger it.

Wire-free alarms

There is now a type of alarm system which does away with the need for wires altogether. It is rather more expensive, but easier to fit, and can move with you from one house to another. It consists of a central processor unit and detection devices which work by using radio waves. Specially selected frequencies are supposed to prevent interference from any other radio-controlled equipment, such as passing taxis, police cars and so on. The system is controlled by a small radio touch-pad about the size of a pocket calculator. It is light and portable so you can control your alarm from any part of the house. As an added bonus, it can be used to activate a personal attack alarm wherever you are – in the house, or outside in the garage or garden.

Alarms linked to a telephone
These should always use a separate, ex-directory telephone line to raise the alarm.

999 autodialler
This device dials 999 and plays a standard pre-recorded message down the phone to the police to say that there's an intruder in house and gives your name, address and phone number. The problem is that some police forces no longer have the manpower to monitor the lines, and so the system is being phased out in certain areas. And of course this system would fail if the burglar cut the lines.

Autodialler
This dials a selected phone number, e.g. a friend or neighbour, and plays a message, which you have to record yourself, informing them that something is wrong and they should phone the police. This has obvious drawbacks: the friend might be out; even if he or she is in, it takes longer for the police to be alerted; as with the 999 autodialler, the system will fail if the line is cut.

Digital communicator
This is a little more sophisticated and costs more. It dials a central monitoring station – usually the burglar alarm company's headquarters. The alarm call comes up on a computer screen which is manned night and day. Staff then immediately alert the police. Unlike the autodialler, which dials its call only once, the digital communicator will try several times, so its message almost always gets through.

   With certain systems, the computer screen will even register any fault on the telephone line. This is a useful facility, because if intruders have cut the wires before breaking in, the police will still be alerted.

This equipment nearly always has to be rented as part of a professionally installed system, and will be subject to regular maintenance inspections by the security company, so it can be quite expensive compared with some of the other systems.

Telecom security
Detectors pick up the first signs of forced entry or fire, and raise the alarm in a central monitoring station which then notifies the relevant emergency service. This system will respond to a fault, and will therefore still work even if the burglars cut the lines. The detectors are easily installed, and the system is wired into a separate outgoing-calls-only telephone line, in the same way as the autodialler and the digital communicator. The initial installation cost is £95 plus VAT, and then a rental of £16.68 is paid monthly. So the total cost in the first year is £278.48, and £200.16 for every year after that. It is expensive, but comprehensive.

The advantage with any of these systems which link up with a central monitoring station is that your home is effectively being 'watched' day and night 365 days a year, whether you're at home or away.

Which alarms are hardest to overcome?
Most alarms will be very difficult for burglars to deactivate, unless they know the system well. As mentioned before, 'self-actuating systems' contain their own batteries so the burglar cannot disarm them by simply cutting the wires to the bell.

Other features to look out for include tamper protection on the sounder box or control panel cover, systems which use stronger four-stranded wire (rather than two-stranded), and contacts which are not easily visible on the surface of window frames, door surrounds, and so on.

24

Panic buttons

Most professionally fitted alarm systems include a panic button or personal attack alarm. Security companies usually recommend that you have two – one by the front door and one by your bed, but you can ask for as many as you like. They are wired to a circuit on the alarm system which is always live, whether or not the alarm has been switched on at the control box. At the first indication that someone is trying to break in, you can simply press the button to sound the alarm. These can be the most comforting feature of any alarm system for someone who feels particularly nervous or vulnerable in the house. One word of caution – don't think the panic button means that you can open the door wide to unexpected callers. Do still use a door chain (see page 109).

The cost of burglar alarms

For an average-sized house, a standard alarm system – consisting of control panel, external sounder box, six magnetic contacts, two space detectors (e.g. PIRs or sound detectors), two panic buttons and pressure mats – will cost between £800 and £900 plus VAT. A digital communicator will be an extra £120 to £150. On top of the initial outlay, there will be the option of a maintenance agreement with the security company which installs the alarm. These maintenance agreements commit you to an annual payment of between £50 and £120, and may also be subject to increase without warning. The more reputable companies usually allow you to opt out of a maintenance contract, and just to call them out when you need them or when you think a service is due. Call-out fees are about £25 a time. A wire-free system, including the special phone connection for central station monitoring, costs around £1200 to install. The relevant British Standard for the wire-free system is BS 6799.

Where should you buy your alarm system?

This is not an easy decision as there are so many different types of system, and different levels of protection, and the security industry has its fair share of cowboy operators ready to make a fast buck by exploiting people's fear of crime. Never buy an alarm system through someone who calls at your door. Before you agree to anything, take advice and compare the prices of at least three other companies for similar systems. This is a highly competitive industry, and you can save yourself a lot of money by shopping around:

● Your first call should be to the Crime Prevention Officer at your local police headquarters. He or she will know the reputable dealers in the area.

● With few exceptions, the reputable dealers belong to one of these three trade organisations: The NSCIA (National Supervisory Council for Intruder Alarms), the BSIA (British Security Industry Association) or the IAAI (Inspectors of Approved Alarm Installers).

● Contact your insurance company to see if they run a discount scheme on your house contents premium if you have an alarm fitted. If so, this will almost certainly depend on using an installer belonging to one of the three organisations mentioned above.

● Even with the reputable companies, do still check the small print, especially where any maintenance agreements are concerned. You may be committing yourself to an indefinite annual fee which can escalate rapidly over the years and may not guarantee you adequate maintenance or servicing anyway.

● There are some good companies around who are not members of the NSCIA, the BSIA or the IAAI, but who offer perfectly acceptable standards of installation at a significantly lower price. Do bear in mind, though, that if you have a complaint about the work that has been done, there is no independent body to support you in any claim you may want to make.

● Whichever company you choose, the alarm should be installed to comply with British Standard 4737, and you should get it in writing that this has been done.

● Each of the companies you approach for quotes will want to visit your home free of charge to assess the kind of system you need. Every house or flat has different security problems, depending on the size of the place, its structure and layout, the area you live in, and the goods you are protecting.

● A good installation should cause your household a minimum of disruption and be relatively tidy. Wires and cables ought to be out of sight, not trailing along the walls or floors. Ask each company how they plan to carry out the work, how long they will take to do it, and how much disruption it will cause.

● Read the last few pages on the different options and devices carefully before you start talking to alarm companies. You get better service when you seem to know what you are talking about!

DIY alarms

You can save yourself up to £400 by installing your own alarm system and it will take you about two days to do. I would only advise doing-it-yourself, however, if you are sure you know what you are doing: firstly for safety reasons, as it involves wiring into the mains electricity; and secondly because, unless the alarm is installed properly, you may end up having too many false alarms – alienating both the neighbours and the police, and ruining the deterrent effect. Alarm manufacturers will usually supply their systems by mail order, or tell you where the nearest stockists are. Do your research on prices, and whatever system you choose, make sure it conforms to British Standard 6707.

It is best to buy from a good security specialist or alarm centre where staff can advise you on installation. The alarm kits all come with instructions of course, but some of them leave quite a lot to be desired in terms of clarity and comprehensibility.

If you are fitting PIRs (Passive Infra-Red Detectors) as part of your system, you should almost certainly get an expert to fit them, as it is absolutely critical to position them correctly if you are to avoid false alarms (see page 20).

As a compromise, you might consider buying the alarm kit yourself from the manufacturer and then finding a good local handyman or electrician to install it for you. There are quite a few now who specialise in this type of job. You will still save money in the short term by buying the alarm kit directly from the manufacturer. However you are less likely to save money on your insurance premium if your alarm has not been professionally installed. If you need any advice at all on fitting alarms, don't forget that your local Crime Prevention Officer will be delighted to help.

Security bars

I personally would be reluctant to live behind bars, but it depends on how much at risk you think you are and the value of the property you have at home. They are rarely necessary in ordinary domestic houses or flats. However, if you have a couple of Monets on the wall, bars are almost certainly a good investment. It is essential that they be fitted by an expert. In the London area, a decorative grille for the average double-pane window would cost at least £80 (including VAT and fitting). Bars would cost even more.

Safes

For goodness sake don't keep large amounts of cash in the house. I never cease to be surprised at the number of burglaries we cover on *Crimewatch* where people – often the elderly – keep all their savings in the house, even though the police are always warning us not to do it.

If you absolutely have to keep large sums at home, then you should invest in a safe. The small underfloor type is best because they are out of sight and can be set in concrete. However, if you live in a flat you'll need a well-concealed wall safe. These cost between £70 and £300, depending on size.

A safe deposit box at the bank costs between £10 and £40 a year, again depending on size.

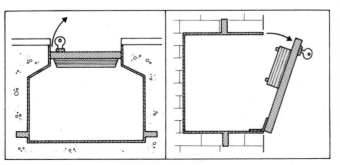

A small floor or wall safe is worth thinking about if you have to keep a lot of cash in the house.

Security lighting

Most burglaries occur when homes are unoccupied so you need to give the would-be thief the impression that someone is in. One of the most effective ways of doing this is simply to keep some lights on, inside and out. It is not a good idea to keep curtains closed or blinds drawn while you are away.

Outside

The first step in security lighting is to fit a porch light over your front and back doors so that a burglar cannot use the cover of darkness to break in unseen. Another good reason to fit a porch light is so that you can see who a caller is before opening the door at night. It is also advisable to put extra lighting at any other points outside the house where an intruder could lurk in the dark. A qualified electrician will charge you around £25 to fit a porch light.

For security lighting to be really effective, the outside lights should be switched on at dusk every single night of the year. Not many people can manage that, but a light-sensitive photocell controller triggered by natural light levels can do it for you. It fits into a light bulb socket and costs between £8 and £12. Or you can wire the lights to a timer switch – and vary the settings occasionally.

For an extra initial outlay of about £90, but to save on the electricity bill in the long run, you can have lights wired to an infra-red detector which reacts to body heat. A burglar will shy away from the sudden flood of light, while a friendly caller will be grateful for the illumination. The lights will remain on as long as there is someone in the vicinity emitting body heat, or for a predetermined time after the source of warmth has gone.

Inside

Make sure there are one or two lights shining from within the house as well, both upstairs and down. These should be on timer switches (costing around £15); or ask a trusted neighbour to go in each night while you are away and turn some lights on – then switch them off later each evening. It is important that indoor lights are left on in living rooms rather than hallways. In fact, lights shining in hallways often indicate that a house is unoccupied. No one actually lives in the hall!

Incidentally, a radio on a timer switch helps add to the illusion that people are at home – preferably tuned to a 'talk' station like BBC Radio 4. Make sure that it is loud enough to be heard, but not so loud that it annoys the neighbours!

Leaving lights on may sound extravagant but it'll actually add up to about £20 extra per year on your electricity bill.

Garage or shed

Garden or DIY tools should never be left lying around the garden for the housebreaker to pick up and use to his advantage. Lock them away in the garage or shed. Always keep any outbuildings locked, as these are often a target for thieves. Some people keep a deep freezer in a building outside – also rich pickings for the casual thief. Never leave ladders lying around either. If you do not have a shed or garage to put them in, chain and padlock them horizontally to a secure fitting on the side of the house.

Padlocks

The most secure padlocks are those operated by a key which opens *and* shuts them. Many of the spring-loaded ones are quite easy to spring open. The best type is a close shackle padlock. As you can see, there isn't enough room to insert an implement to lever it open. These cost about £30. The open shackle padlock is less secure, but if you do go for one of these, make sure it's a good-quality one, which will cost about £15.

LEFT: an open shackle padlock
RIGHT: a close shackle padlock which is more difficult to open.

Fitting a padlock bar ('padbars')

Ideally you should use coach bolts rather than screws, but if you do use screws, they should be 'clutch-headed' or one-way screws which, once in, are almost impossible to remove.

If you use ordinary screws, spoil the slot afterwards with a screwdriver to achieve the same effect. In addition, you can obscure the screw heads with plastic wood, putty or whatever is appropriate. Padbars which completely cover the fixings are also available.

A more expensive but very secure concealed shackle padlock – and no screw-heads to get at on the padbar.

When you are fitting any kind of lock or bolt, do use good tough screws. It is no use fitting marvellous expensive locks and then installing them with weak screws; one blow and it's a break-in!

Other precautions

● Don't give a would-be intruder any opportunity to work unobserved. Keep hedges low in front and at the side of the house. Fences should be low or see-throughable! Shrubs and trees near the house should be trimmed well back.

● Dustbins can be used to climb on. Keep them somewhere conspicuous, and away from vulnerable windows, extension roofs and so on.

● A coat of slippery anti-climb paint, available from DIY and paint shops at about £11 for 2.5 litres, will render the drainpipes useless to a burglar – and leave tell-tale marks on his clothing. Remember though, to avoid losing any friends, apply the paint above the level at which legitimate callers can accidentally rub against it!

● Try to position valuables (like the television set, video recorder, hi-fi and so on) in such a way that they are not temptingly visible through the windows. LED readouts and digital clocks, for instance, can be particularly eye-catching.

● When you are going to be away, you will probably remember to cancel the milk and the newspapers, but ask someone to keep an eye out for any bulky mail, trade papers or circulars which might be left sticking out of the letter box. Make sure that heaps of mail building up on the doormat are not going to be visible from outside.

● In spring and summer, if you have a garden, cut the lawn just before you go on holiday. If you are away for more than a week ask someone to mow it for you. Long grass can be a real giveaway. So can dry drains! Ask the neighbour to run the taps for a minute or so each day.

● Keep the house keys in a safe place – *not* under the mat, beneath a flower pot or on a string behind the letter box. Crime Prevention Officers stress that keys should not be hidden outside your house or flat under any circumstances.

● Give a spare key to a trusted neighbour. If you have a burglar alarm, you must nominate another keyholder besides yourself and inform the police who that person is.

● A dog is a good deterrent to burglars, but if you don't have one, a BEWARE OF THE DOG sign on the gate can be a help. Some people even go as far as keeping a kennel and a food bowl in the garden!

● Display stickers prominently in the windows to show that you are a member of any Neighbourhood Watch or Home Watch scheme, and to advertise the fact that your property is security marked.

Property marking

Once your home is broken into, there is a less than one-in-three chance that the burglar will be caught, and unless your property is marked with your postcode, there's even less chance of you ever seeing it again. A sticker in your window telling the would-be thief that your property has been marked is a deterrent in itself. He will then know that if he steals from you, not only will it be difficult for him to sell the goods, but they will also be traceable, which means a greater risk of his being caught. As regular viewers of *Crimewatch* will know, almost every police station has a veritable Aladdin's cave of unclaimed stolen goods waiting to be collected by their rightful owners. Several burglaries have been cleared up as a result of viewers spotting long-lost treasures on the programme.

Anything that's marked permanently with postcodes and names and addresses I steered clear of – it just wasn't worth the hassle. I like the idea of people putting stickers in their windows advertising that their property was marked. It saved me from wasting my time.

There are two basic types of property marking – visible and invisible.

Visible marking

Permanent, visible marking is always best wherever possible because it acts as a deterrent in itself. You can use ceramic markers or diamond-tipped engravers. The ceramic markers are designed for glass, china, vitreous enamel or any hard glazed finish. A special metal compound is deposited as a permanent mark without scratching or cutting into the surface.

These markers usually come complete with a stencil. Diamond-tipped engravers are ideal for hard objects like gold, silver, other metals, plastic and polished wood. Both types of marker can be used to etch your car registration number on the windows (see page 66). If you mark antiques or certain other valuables with these, you may detract from their value, although it sometimes enhances the value of an object if you can trace its history through its markings. If you have any doubts, check with experts such as Christie's or Sotheby's.

Property marking: hard or metal objects are best marked with a diamond-tipped engraving pen.

Heavier items such as lawn mowers, and other tools and machinery can be stamped with a quarter-inch die and a small hammer which are available with a set of letters and numbers so that you can imprint your code. Some bicycles can be marked in this way too (see page 83).

There are also electrically operated engravers which can be used on hard surfaces including glass. These are stocked by most DIY chains and some discount shops, and cost between £20 and £26.

Invisible marking

Invisible marking, using ultra-violet markers, is not permanent, and therefore not as effective. It has to be renewed approximately every two years, or more often if it has been exposed to strong sunlight, dry-cleaning or polishing. This type of marking is for belongings, such as antiques, documents or clothing, on which you do not want the marks to show. Just one cautionary note here for people who own compact discs: *never* mark the discs themselves with ultra-violet. You won't be able to play them any more! Just mark the plastic cases.

The best way of identifying your valuables is by marking them with your postcode, which represents about twenty houses or flats in a street. If you add your house number to that, you have your own unique code: e.g. W12 8QT 24. If and when you move house, mark an X after your old code, and add the new one next to it.

If you do not know your postcode, you can find it in your *Thomson Local Directory*, or telephone the local postcode information section which is listed in the telephone directory under 'Post Office Services' or ask at your main post office.

Complete property-marking kits (including ceramic marker, diamond-tipped engraver, fabric marker, ultra-violet marker and warning labels) are available in some good stationery shops, ironmongers, DIY shops and specialist security firms for around £6. A kit is much better value than buying any of the markers individually. Even better, the Crime Prevention Officer at your local police station will probably be able to lend you a kit, or, if you belong to a Neighbourhood Watch Scheme, you will be able to borrow one through that.

NB: You should ask permission before marking any equipment that has been rented, such as television sets and video recorders.

Keeping records

Make a list of your valuable possessions together with an estimate of what each item is worth. You should also make a note of everything you own that has a serial number, and keep the list of numbers in a safe place.

Photograph any distinctive valuables and anything you cannot mark, such as jewellery and antiques. Include a ruler in each photo to give an accurate idea of scale and pay special attention to any distinguishing features, such as hallmarks, crests or initials.

It's a good idea to leave the negatives and a copy of your list at a different address with a responsible friend or relative. And don't forget to use the free window stickers which your Crime Prevention Officer will provide. A burglar will think twice about stealing anything he knows has been coded.

Police recommend the best means of marking various individual items as follows:

Cameras and binoculars	Ultra-violet on inside, etch casing, or both.
China or porcelain	Ultra-violet on base, or ceramic marker or photograph.
Clocks (metal)	Etch with scribe on base or casing. If unusual or distinctive design, photograph.
Clocks (wood)	Ultra-violet inside casing. Etching is possible but you may risk damaging the wood. Photograph.
Clothes (e.g. leather jackets)	Spirit-based ultra-violet pen or fabric marker.

39

Cycles	Usually done by police or cycle shop. Photograph if distinctive.
Glass	Not really suitable for marking, but can use ultra-violet or etching *fluid*. Photograph.
Gold, silver, precious metals	Photograph is best, or you could etch with scribe, or mark with ultra-violet, remembering that polishing will remove it.
Handbags	Use ball-point pen on inside. Full name and address not advisable. Postcode is enough.
Jewellery	Most small items are not suitable for marking. Some can be etched. Photograph is best, or jeweller may advise.
Ladders	Etch with scribe, or paint.
Lawnmowers	Use marking punches, or etch with scribe, or paint.
Paintings	Ultra-violet on back of canvas and photograph.
TV, video, radio, hi-fi equipment	Scribe plastic or metal surface on rear or base. *If rented check with company first.*
Watches	Etch with scribe on the back.

NB: Always take expert advice before you mark antiques or valuable jewellery.

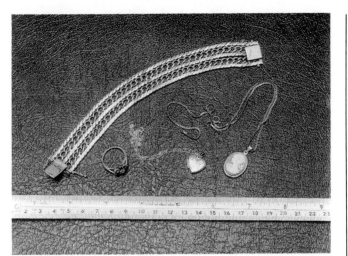

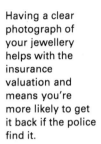

Having a clear photograph of your jewellery helps with the insurance valuation and means you're more likely to get it back if the police find it.

Police often advise using a Polaroid camera to photograph your valuables. Apparently it is not un-known for someone working at a developers and printers to be a security risk! Your local police can usually put you in touch with a professional security photographer if you like.

Don't forget that ultra-violet fades especially quickly in direct sunlight. Painting over the mark with polyurethane varnish will prevent this happening.

Valuable property record		
Item	Value	Serial no.

Use this chart to record details of your valuables.

Reporting something suspicious

If you see or hear anything that makes you think a crime is being committed, even if you are not sure whether it constitutes an emergency, always dial 999 and ask for the police. If it turns out to be a false alarm, you will still have done the right thing. The police always emphasise that it is better to be safe than sorry.

When you get through to the police, tell them your name and give them the address and telephone number you are calling from. *Stay where you are.* The police advise us not to try to approach any suspects, but to wait and keep watching what happens until the police arrive on the scene.

It is worth everyone in the family memorising exactly where the 9 is on the telephone dial, in case you should ever have to dial 999 in the dark for some reason. Remember that 9 is the last but one digit on the circular dial. On a push-button phone, the 9 is on the far right and one up from the bottom.

If you want to report something that you feel is not an emergency but is worrying you—perhaps you haven't seen any sign of a neighbour for a couple of days, the milk is building up on the doorstep and you think the police should check on the situation, or if you simply need some Crime Prevention advice, then contact your Neighbourhood Watch co-ordinator, if you belong to a scheme, or phone your local police station.

Make sure you keep these numbers by the phone for everyone in your house to refer to:

LOCAL POLICE STATION	
LOCAL BEAT OFFICER	
CRIME PREVENTION OFFICER	
NEIGHBOURHOOD WATCH	
DOCTOR	

Giving a good description

One of the difficulties and frustrations the police face is being given poor descriptions of people or vehicles at the scene of crimes. Many promising investigations have failed because of vague descriptions from witnesses.

No matter how observant you think you are, it's worth testing yourself. Try to describe someone who has just walked past you in the street and see how well you do. You may be surprised at how little detail you have actually retained. I recently shocked myself at how vague I sounded when I tried to give my local police a description of a man I'd seen behaving suspiciously. Since then I have been practising my powers of observation as I walk or drive around. The trick is not to try to form an overall impression of something or someone you have seen. You will only become daunted and confused if you try to remember everything. Look out for a few basic and specific characteristics. I have listed the most important ones below. It often helps to compare a person with yourself or someone you know by asking yourself questions, such as how much taller was he than I am? Was he older or younger than my brother/father etc?

Of a person

Male or female?

Colour of skin?

Complexion: dark or fair?
          clean-shaven or bearded?
          spotty or clear?

Height: tall or short?

Build: thickset or slim?

Age: young, middle-aged or old?

Spectacles or not?

43

Hair: curly or straight?
     long or short?
     dark or fair?
     thick or receding?

Face: long? thin? round? fat?

Marks: tattoos? scars?

Clothing: light or dark?
         casual or smart?

Hat?

Voice: deep or not?
     accent?

Carrying anything?

Anything distinctive or unusual?

Of a car/van/lorry/motorcycle/bicycle

Registration number?

Colour?

Make: Ford, Vauxhall etc?

Model: Cortina, Nova etc?

Old or new-looking?

Two-door or four-door?

Saloon, estate or hatchback?

Any distinctive features: paintwork? rust? dents?
                  stripes or transfers?
                  company name?

Direction in which it drove off?

Neighbourhood Watch

The most likely targets for burglary are not houses in well-to-do areas, but homes in less privileged residential districts. Semi-detached and end-of-terrace houses, maisonettes and council estates are much more popular with thieves than bigger, richer-looking houses. This is why those who can least afford it often have to pay most in insurance premiums. You are also much more likely to be burgled in an inner-city area than in a village or small town. The most recent Home Office figures show the highest-risk counties in the UK to be Merseyside, Northumbria and Greater Manchester. At lowest risk are Surrey, Hertfordshire, Dyfed and Powys. Most burglaries occur on weekdays in homes where the occupants are out, and there are as many break-ins in broad daylight as there are at night.

Of course the ideal would be to have a police officer watching every house in every residential street every minute of the day and night, but as inner-city populations continue to rise and police resources become increasingly stretched, this is obviously quite out of the question. The traditional image of the local bobby on the beat – who knows everyone on his patch *and* their children's names, who often drops into people's houses for a cup of tea and a chat, does the odd bit of shopping for some of the elderly folk *and* has a shrewd idea of who the local no-gooders are – is disappearing fast. Instead, we have to recognise that, whereas there cannot be a police officer at every gate, there can be a neighbour. In fact we usually know far more about our own neighbourhood than anyone from outside. A police officer seeing someone in your garden, for example, might not recognise him or her as a stranger, but your neighbour probably would. The fact that we have this specialised knowledge, and that we are much more likely to thwart the criminal if we help each other, has

Postcode	Risk of burglary
AB3–5	1
B93, 94	3
B28, 30, 31, 37, 43, 44 46, 47, 69–75, 90–92, 98	4
B23, 26, 27, 32–36, 38, 45, 66–68	5
B14, 17, 20, 24, 25, 29	6
B1–9, 13, 15, 16, 21	7
B10	8
B11, 12, 18, 19	9
BB3–7, 9, 12	3
BB1, 2	4
BB8, 10, 11	5
FY4, 8	4
FY1–3, 6, 7	5
BL6, 8	4
BL7, 9	5
BL0, 1–5	6
BH1–3, 5, 7, 8	3
BD6, 7, 14–17, 21	4
BD1–3, 8, 10, 12, 13, 18–20	5
BD4, 5, 9	6
BN1, 2	5
BN3	6
BS3, 12	3
BS1, 2, 4, 7–11	4
BS5, 6	5
BR4, 6, 8	5
BR2, 5	6
BR1, 3, 7	7
CB1–11	1
CT4, 5, 7, 9, 10, 12	3
CF4	4
CF1–3, 5, 6	5
	1
CM11–15, 17, 18, 20–24	3
CM16, 19	4
CH1–6, 8	4
CV3–6	3
CV1, 2, 7	5
CW1–3, 5–7, 9–12	3
CW4, 8	4
CR2, 3	5
CR0, 4	6
DL15	3
DL1, 3, 5, 6, 13, 14, 16, 17	4
DA7, 9–12	4
DA1–6, 8, 15–18	5
DA13, 14	6
DN1–12, 15	3
DY1–4, 6, 9	3
DY8	4
DD1–11	1
DH1–3, 9	3
DH4–8	4
EH2, 3, 9, 10, 12–14 18–25, 54	4
EH1, 4–8, 11, 15–17	5
EN6, 10, 11	4
EN7–9	5
EN2, 4, 5	6
En1, 3	7
EX7–16, 19–30, 32–36	1
TD1–15	1
G63, 65, 66, 84	4
G60–62, 67–69, 74–78, 82	5
G11–14, 31, 32, 44, 46, 52, 64, 71, 73, 81, 83	6

Postcode	Risk of burglary
G20, 22, 23, 33, 41, 43	7
G1–5	8
G15, 21, 34, 40, 42, 45, 51, 53, 72	9
GU5–10, 16, 17, 25, 26, 31	4
HX1–7	3
HG2, 3, 5	3
HA2, 4	5
HA0, 1, 3, 5, 6, 9	7
HA7, 8	8
HR1–9	1
HD1–8	3
IG1–11	6
IV1–56	1
IP6–33	1
PO30–41	1
KA27	1
KT23, 24	3
KT12–16, 18, 19, 21	4
KT3–9, 11, 17, 20, 22	5
KT1, 2, 10	6
KW1–17	1
LS11, 15, 19	3
LS21–28	4
LS12, 13, 17, 18, 20, 29	5
LS1–6, 9, 14, 16	6
LS7, 8, 10	7
LE2, 3	3
L39	4
L37, 38, 40, 64, 66	5
L23, 29–31, 45–49 60–63, 65	6
L22, 25–27, 34–36, 44	8
L1–21, 24, 28, 32, 33, 41–43	9
LD1–8	1
LL23–78	1
London	
E4, 18	6
E6, 10, 11, 17	8
E1–3, 5, 7–9, 12–16	9
EC1–4	8
N21	7
N2, 6, 8, 9, 11–14, 20	8
N1, 3–5, 7, 10, 15–19, 22	9
NW1, 2, 5–7, 9, 10	8
NW3, 4, 8, 11	9
SE9, 20, 25	7
SE1–4, 6, 7, 10–12, 14 18, 19, 21–24, 26, 28	8
SE5, 8, 13, 15–17, 27	9
SW6, 13–15, 19, 20	7
SW1, 3–5, 7, 10–12, 16–18	8
SW2, 8, 9	9
W3–7, 12, 13	7
W1, 8, 11, 14	8
W2, 9, 10	9
WC1, 2	8
LU1–7	3
M29	4
M26, 27, 30, 34, 35	5
M18, 19, 24, 28, 31, 32	6
M9, 17, 22, 25, 33	7
M10, 20, 21, 23	8
M1–8, 11–16	9
ME3, 14	3
ME4, 5, 11–13, 18	4
ME7, 9, 15, 17	5
MK1–16	3
ML1–11	5

Postcode	Risk of burglary
NE18, 43, 44, 48, 49, 61	3
NE12, 13, 16, 17, 20, 23 28, 33–36, 41, 45–47, 62–65	4
NE7, 9, 21, 26, 27, 29–32 37, 40, 42	5
NE1, 3, 8, 15, 38, 39	6
NE2, 5, 6, 10, 11	7
NE4	8
BT1–10, 16, 18–33, 37–47, 49	3
Bt11–15, 17, 34–36, 48	5
NR9–30, 32–35	1
NG1, 7	4
OL2, 3, 6–8, 10, 13	5
OL1, 4, 5, 9, 11, 12, 15, 16	6
PA26–88	1
PA6–15	4
PA4, 5	5
PA1–3	6
PH1–44	1
PL10–35	1
PR1–3, 5, 7	3
PR4, 6	4
PR8, 9	5
RH1–5, 8, 9, 13, 14, 17	4
RM4, 12, 14	5
RM1–3, 5–11, 13	6
S9, 11, 13, 14, 63, 66, 71–75	3
S1–5, 65	4
S7, 70	5
ZE1–3	1
SY15–25	1
SL0, 1–4, 6, 9	4
SL5, 7	5
SO1, 2	3
SS11–14, 16, 17	3
SK12, 14–17	4
SK1–10	5
SR6–8	4
SR1–5	5
SM1–7	5
SA19–67	1
SA1, 2, 4–7	4
TA12–24	1
TS7, 8, 19–26	4
TS1–6	5
TN31–35, 39	3
TN3, 6–8, 13–17, 21, 22	4
TQ6–14	1
TR1–27	1
TW15–20	4
TW1–14	5
UB7–10	4
UB4, 5	6
UB3	7
UB2, 6	8
UB1	9
WF1–17	3
WS1–5	3
WA1, 4–6, 8, 12	4
WA2, 3, 7, 9–11, 16	5
WA13–15	6
WD1, 3, 4	4
WD2	5
WD6, 7	6
WN5, 6	4
WN1–4, 7, 8	5
WV1–6, 12–14	4

formed the basis of the Neighbourhood Watch schemes – sometimes known as Home Watch or Community Watch.

Most of us will ask the neighbours to keep an eye on our home when we go away, and that helps to give us peace of mind for those two weeks or so. With a Neighbourhood Watch scheme operating, you should have that sense of security all the time – whether you are out at work all day or just popping out to the shops.

Since the idea first came to the UK in 1982, the number of schemes has increased dramatically to more than 50 000. On the whole they seem to be most successful in middle-class areas, and have been criticised for simply driving the criminals to other streets nearby which don't have a Watch scheme. However, they certainly seem to have had an overall deterrent effect on residential burglary and on thefts of and from cars. Some areas claim a 50 per cent reduction in house break-ins.

> *Personally, I reckon that the nosey neighbour is the burglar's worst enemy, and if these schemes take off it could put a few of my colleagues out of work – if you know what I mean.*

How to set up a watch scheme

Sometimes it is the police who suggest setting up a scheme and sometimes it is the residents who approach the police asking for help in starting one. Then everyone in the group who is interested will meet and choose one or more co-ordinators. For obvious reasons, these are usually people who spend most of their time at home. Their job is to liaise between the members of the scheme and the local police, and to be ready to pass on information from the neighbours about anything suspicious they may have seen or heard. (Obviously, if something needs urgent and

Look up your postcode on the chart opposite to see how high your risk of being burgled is: 1 is low, 9 is high. All post codes *not* listed here are class 2.

immediate attention – if a resident sees someone in the act of breaking into a neighbour's home for example – one should still dial 999 at once.) The co-ordinators, or sometimes the local beat officers, will circulate a regular newsletter to all the members of the scheme. This will contain information such as descriptions of particular burglars known to be operating in the area, or perhaps of a new ploy some conmen are trying on householders, and there will also be Crime Prevention tips and advice.

Meetings will be called every so often by the co-ordinators to keep the residents in touch with each other. It is usually at the first or second meeting that the Crime Prevention Officer will demonstrate how to mark your property with your postcode. This is partly so that you stand a better chance of getting your property back if you are burgled, and partly as a deterrent to theft in the first place because the thief will know the items are traceable and difficult to sell

Just having a Neighbourhood Watch sticker in your window may be enough to deter a thief.

(see page 36 on property marking). The officer will usually be able to lend the scheme a property-marking kit and will make sure everyone has stickers to advertise both that they are members of a Neighbourhood Watch scheme and that their property has been marked. Valuable deterrents!

Through the Watch scheme, you can also arrange for the Crime Prevention Officer to visit your home for a free security survey. He or she can show you the points where your home might be vulnerable to break-ins, recommend types of lock or alarm system you might consider fitting and give you the names of the best local dealers and installers. This service is available to everyone free of charge, whether you belong to a Watch scheme or not.

One more advantage of belonging to a Watch scheme is that together you have greater power in negotiations with the local authority on any improvements you would like made to the area to reduce the risk of crime – such as better street lighting or changing the position of a bus stop.

The elderly at risk

As we often say on *Crimewatch*, it is a fact that elderly people are less likely to be the victims of crime than any other section of the community, although this sometimes is hard to believe when it is crimes against the elderly and children that hit the headlines and shock us most. It is, however, also true to say that old people can sometimes be more vulnerable to crime. Their habits are more predictable; they are often unable to afford the best security locks and alarm systems; and some people, who grew up in the days before personal bank accounts and cheque books, keep quite large sums of money in the house, under the mattress or in a teapot.

This is why the elderly are prime targets for con-men – who pretend to be from the Water Board, the Gas Board, the local council or even the police. These utterly unscrupulous people will use all kinds of official-sounding identities and excuses to gain entrance into homes, and once in, they know exactly where to look for those 'hidden' valuables or savings.

So my appeal is, *please* keep your cash in a building society, post office or bank and – even more important – do not let anyone into your home unless you are sure they are who they say they are. Use that door chain or door limiter. You don't have to let anyone into your house if you do not want to. Just tell them you'll call their office to make an appointment at another time when it is more convenient for you. And when you telephone their office, look up the number in the phone book rather than using the number on any printed card they may put through the letter box. See page 106 for more advice on dealing with suspicious callers.

As for help with security measures, some local councils provide a security grant of about £40 to pensioners for locks and bolts, and they will arrange for the locks to be fitted free. If your council does not have a scheme like that, your local Help the Aged or

Age Concern branch will tell you what financial assistance is available, and in many areas they run schemes of their own. Both these organisations, and some other bodies like the WRVS and the Round Table, raise funds especially to buy alarms for elderly people. One of the largest crime prevention organisations in the country now is NACRO – the National Association for the Care and Resettlement of Offenders – which has a separate division, quite apart from that concerned with ex-offenders, entirely devoted to crime prevention. If, for example, there is a need for door chains or limiters to be fitted in the homes of the elderly people in a particular area, then the nearest local branch of NACRO may be willing to fit them free of charge. They will be able to tell you about one particular type of alarm which is activated by pressing a button on the telephone, or by pulling on a pendant worn around the neck. This device is a kind of two-way radio by which you can speak to a particular relative or friend, or to someone at a communications centre (manned 24 hours a day) who can talk to you, offer reassurance or advice if you need it, or summon immediate help from the police or ambulance service.

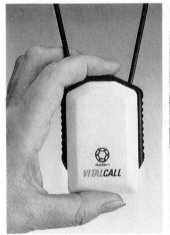

For elderly people living on their own, help can be only minutes away with either (left) a pendant alarm or (right) a wall-mounted alarm activated by a cord. Check to see if grants are available.

51

What to do if you are burgled

● Keep calm, don't panic. Dial 999 as soon as you can.

● Don't go in if you think the intruder or intruders may still be there. Leave quickly and quietly and phone the police from a neighbour's home or from a phone box.

● If you see the burglar, try to get a good look at him. The police will need a description of him (see page 43). Watch which way he goes. If he gets into a vehicle, try to note the registration number, colour, make and any distinctive dents or paintwork.

● Once you are sure it is safe to go in, the police advice is not to touch anything in case you destroy valuable forensic evidence. This is not always easy because, although in most cases the police will arrive fairly promptly, in some of the very busy city areas it can take them as long as 24 hours to reach you. If this is the case, you'll want to clear up any mess, but be prepared to give the police as many details as you can over the phone and ask them if it is all right to tidy up.

● Take the name of the officer who calls on you, or speaks to you on the phone. You may want to speak to him or her again with additional information, or to find out how the investigation is going.

● While you are waiting for the police to arrive, try to assess what is missing as best you can without disturbing anything. If you have marked your property and kept photos and records of valuables, serial numbers and so on, this should not be too difficult.

● Try to find out how the intruder broke in.

● If you belong to a Neighbourhood Watch Scheme, tell the co-ordinator what has happened. Someone may have seen something, and it will also warn the rest of the street about the burglar.

Part of the distress of being burgled is the mess the intruder often leaves behind.

● Arrange for any broken locks, windows or doors to be repaired as soon as possible. Many security companies and locksmiths offer 24-hour service. And check whether any keys have gone.

● You should report the loss of any credit cards, cheque books, post office books, vehicle registration documents or any other important papers to the relevant authorities and the police as soon as you can.

● Notify your insurance company and ask them to send a claim form.

● Make a list of missing valuables and serial numbers. Send a copy to your insurance company, and give another one to the police.

● If you hear an intruder while you are in your home, don't try to tackle him. Most burglars will flee empty-handed rather than risk a confrontation. Instead, try moving about and making a lot of noise. Switch lights on and off, and maybe even call out to an (imaginary) companion. It's a good idea to have a phone extension in your bedroom and a list of emergency numbers to hand so that you can phone quickly and quietly if you are disturbed in the night.

If the worst should happen and you do come face to face with an intruder there's advice in Section 3 on how to keep your head and handle the situation.

> *A friend of mine, a very old lady, was surprised by a burglar in her house. Now she's very sweet and quite religious too and she just said 'Oh, you poor man! What a terrible life you must have to have come to this . . .' I can just see her doing it too. Absolutely genuine, of course. You could never fake something like that. Anyway I think he must have been stunned. She asked him to pray with her but he apologised and left . . . amazing!*

Victims Support

Many people who have been burgled feel the need to talk to someone. In most cases of domestic burglary the police will notify the nearest Victims Support Scheme. These are wonderful people who work as volunteers and will give you moral support and practical advice whenever they are needed. The police may also contact them after a mugging, a rape or any offences concerning elderly people. There are now over 300 schemes around the UK, serving about two-thirds of the population, and the National Association of Victims Support Schemes hopes to be able to cover the whole of the UK by the early 1990s.

They can give practical help such as arranging for emergency glaziers or locksmiths to call and repair damage, or filling in that complex insurance claim form and helping to assess what is missing. After crimes of violence, they can assist with legal action involving claims for compensation. Their aim is to take the fear out of crime, and nothing is too much trouble for these volunteers. They also know exactly what sort of emotional help might be needed, and can be of great comfort. They are familiar with the full range of emotional reactions that are usual after a burglary:

● Why has this happened to me?

● Some people feel physically sick – almost as though it is they and not the house which has been violated.

● Anger at the intruder or at society in general for allowing it to happen, or at yourself or someone else for inadequate attention to security.

● You may be very upset at losing some item of particular sentimental value.

● Shock and disgust at all the mess.

● Annoyance and frustration because the police may seem rather nonchalant about what has happened to you and there is nothing you can do about it yourself.

● You may feel frightened that you will be burgled again, although statistically this is highly unlikely, and will perhaps feel suspicious of genuine callers such as neighbours and tradesmen.

● You are likely to want to clean the house throughout, and perhaps change some of the furniture around. Some people even want to move house.

If, for some reason, a local Victims Support Scheme does not get in touch with someone who has suffered a burglary or any other type of crime, then it is easy to find them. Your local police or the nearest Citizens' Advice Bureau will tell you, or you can contact the National Association of Victims Support Schemes, 17a Electric Lane, London SW9 8LA (Tel: 01 326 1084). They would love to hear from any would-be volunteers too!

Insurance

These days many insurance companies offer discounts of up to 15 per cent on your house contents premium if you take certain security measures, such as:

● installing an approved burglar alarm

● installing a safe if you have to keep large amounts of cash at home

● fitting good locks on doors and windows

● joining a Neighbourhood Watch Scheme

If possible, it's better to contact your insurance company *before* you install new alarms, locks or safes to make sure of what discounts they offer. Perhaps you could get a better deal from another company? Some insurance companies have reciprocal arrangements with security firms, so that is worth checking too. Insurance companies vary enormously in the premiums they charge and in what their policies cover, so it is worth making several phone calls to find out which offers the best deal.

Make sure you are properly insured – not only against burglary but also against *attempted* burglary and criminal damage as well. For example, if your patio doors are badly damaged in an attempted break-in the repair is likely to be quite costly, but your insurance company won't be liable to pay you anything unless you have specifically insured against criminal damage *as well as* burglary – in fact you might have been better off being burgled! If you live near a football ground or a rowdy pub, you might also be well advised to insure your home against criminal damage.

Of course, once your home has been burgled, and you have made a claim on your insurance, your premium is likely to go up. So do make sure you fit all your crime prevention devices *now*.

Making a list of your property

If you are like most people, insurance is something you really only think about when you have to make a claim – and that is the moment of truth when you find out whether or not you are adequately covered. Most people are not. Reading all the small print in the policy document, and making a systematic list of your property is pretty tedious, but I can only say that it is well worth setting aside an evening to do it. Choose a time when there is nothing much on the telly, get your husband or wife or a good friend to help, pour yourselves a cup of tea or a glass of wine and go round the house, room by room, writing down every item that is worth more than £50. Don't forget the garage and the garden shed. Garden tools and furniture can add up to a fair amount, and so can the contents of a freezer.

Add up the total value of all the items you have noted, plus an estimate for all items under £50 – like the electric kettle, the hair dryer, clocks, watches and so on. The contents of an average three-bedroomed home can come to between £16 000 and £17 000, but most people are not insured for anything like that. The catch is that if your estimate is too low, the compensation from your insurance company will be reduced according to the amount by which you were under-insured. If your estimate is too high, then you simply receive however much is needed to cover what you have lost.

Most of us arrange our insurance when we move house and then forget about it. If we add any improvements or extensions to the house, we're unlikely to remember to phone the insurance company to tell them. The cost of replacing a fitted kitchen will go up quite considerably. Have you received any special presents or bought anything new recently? A television perhaps, or a washing machine? A smart new watch? Ideally, every time you acquire something new, you should inform your insurers straight

| **Typical house contents record**

Most insurance companies will provide you with a chart like this on which to tot up the value of your possessions. Be sure to do this properly every year when you renew your premium, tedious chore though it is, or you may find you're seriously under-insured.

CHECK LIST	Lounge	Dining Room	Kitch
Carpets, rugs and floorcoverings			
Furniture and furnishings e.g. tables, chairs, stools, suites, curtains and their fittings, cushions, pictures, lighting, non-portable TVs, radios and hi-fi, etc.			
Household appliances e.g. cooker, washing machine, fridge/freezer, vacuum cleaner, electrical goods, heating units/fuel, etc.			
Cooking utensils, provisions and miscellaneous items e.g. cutlery, china/crockery, household silver, glass, food* and drink, fuel, books, etc.			
Garden and garage equipment e.g. lawnmowers, garden furniture, tools, ladders, paints, etc.			
Clothing (excluding furs)			
Household linen e.g. bedding, towels, table linen, etc.			
Valuables e.g. gold and silver articles (excluding household silver), furs, jewellery, watches, clocks, ornaments, cameras, portable TVs/hi-fi/radios, collections, etc.			
Leisure/pastimes e.g. sports equipment, cycles, toys, musical instruments, records and tapes, etc.			
Other items (including money, subject to policy limit)			

* Your policy may require you to pay extra for freezer contents

all airs ding	Main Bedroom	2nd Bedroom	3rd Bedroom	Bathroom /Toilets	Garage and Out-buildings	**TOTALS**

TOTAL

away – and the list should certainly be updated every year when renewing the policy. Many insurers link their contents premiums with the retail price index, but you should still allow for the fact that some items will have appreciated in value – antique furniture, jewellery, will be worth more than they were the year before. Talking of presents, some insurance companies will provide extra cover during weddings or over the Christmas period when you have more things of value than usual at home.

Making a claim

We all think that insurance companies will do anything to wriggle out of paying out their precious money, and that is probably true; but it really is up to us to read the small print from the start and find out exactly what is and is not covered. Did you know, for example, that valuable documents such as deeds, securities, investment bonds and manuscripts usually have to be insured separately? Or that most policies exclude insurance coverage if your house is unoccupied for more than 30 consecutive days? If you're likely to go off on a long holiday or business trip, take note! Your insurance may also be void if you are burgled through an unlocked window or door, or if you left a spare key outside.

There are enormous variations between companies in what their standard policies cover and the premiums they charge. Most insurers decide the premiums by postcodes, and the rates can vary greatly from one postcode to the next. Get quotations from as many different companies as you can – you could make quite a significant saving on your premium. One good thing is that the insurance market is now so competitive that companies are trying much harder to win our business with special offers and inducements. They certainly offer a lot more advice and information these days, and many of them are at last realising that their policies are much easier to sell if they are written in plain English! If you need any help in making a claim you can hire your own loss assessor who will charge you 10 per cent of the eventual claim.

For any general help or advice – especially tips on what to include on your contents list and how to value particular items – the Association of British Insurers, which represents the industry as a whole, will be glad to help. Telephone or write to the Association of British Insurers, Public Affairs Department, Aldermary House, Queen Street, London EC4N 1TT (Tel: 01 248 4477).

Section 2

Vehicle security

A car-thief's delight: 1) back door unlocked; 2) window not wound up properly; 3) tempting briefcase left in full view; 4) no window etching or alarm sticker; 5) pay-as-you-leave parking slip left in the car.

Theft of and from cars – 'autocrime' the police call it – is one and a half times more common than house burglary. It is the most common by far of all the types of crime reported to the police, who reckon that one car is broken into every 20 seconds in Great Britain.

Unfortunately, most car manufacturers have only recently begun to take security more seriously, and the majority of cars on the road present little challenge to the thief. At the same time though, there is more gadgetry available now than ever before to keep the thief away.

Like house burglary, roughly 80 per cent of all thefts involving cars are unplanned opportunist crimes. In many cases, cars are broken into or stolen, simply because the owner has forgotten to lock one of the doors or the boot. This is very easily done unless you make it a matter of absolute habit to check all the locks and windows every time you leave the car – even if you only plan to be away for a minute or two and even if the car is parked in your own driveway or garage. All the windows should be closed completely. The smallest gap gives the thief the opportunity he needs.

Thefts *from* cars

Without realising it, people often almost invite crime. Take a look along a line of parked cars in any ordinary street. The odds are that you'll see something of value in two out of every five: cameras, coats, binoculars, tool-kits, cassette tapes, even cheque books and wallets – left lying casually on seats, parcel shelves or dashboards, and offering irresistible temptation to any passing thief, especially if there is no sign of an alarm system.

Obviously, valuables should not be left in the car at all, but if this is unavoidable for some reason, lock them away out of sight in the boot, or keep an old blanket in the car to cover them up. If a thief is not sure that breaking into your car is worthwhile he is likely to move on to the next one. By leaving *any* articles (valuable or not) where they can be seen, you are inviting trouble – and bear in mind that less than a tenth of all property stolen from cars is ever recovered.

When you are buying something valuable like a television set, don't buy it and then leave it in the car while you do some more shopping. Leave it at the shop until you are ready to collect it, put it straight into the car and drive home. Remember that loading and unloading is usually permitted on double yellow lines. And on a long journey bear in mind that motorway service stations provide rich pickings for thieves because so many of us leave baggage visible or unattended on the roof rack when we leave the car for that much-needed tea break.

Car radios, stereo systems, CB sets and car telephones are all obvious targets for thieves so, if you can, take equipment like this with you when you leave the car, or lock it in the boot. As this often isn't possible, however, you can only try to hide or disguise it. Some manufacturers are now taking this problem into account. One system has a fold-down plastic cover which completely hides the cassette/radio when it's not being used. Some makes have a security code which you key in when the radio is fitted. If the radio is then removed, it will not work unless the correct code is keyed in again. Other makes lock into place automatically when the car's ignition is turned off or when the driver's door is locked. If you have any of these devices, put a sticker in the window to say so – otherwise your car may still be broken into and damaged before the thief finds out that his efforts will go unrewarded. I hope more manufacturers will soon become enlightened enough to follow some of these examples.

Don't forget that petrol is worth money too. It's

easily siphoned out of the tank unless you have a locking petrol cap, which costs about £5 – a worthwhile investment. It will also prevent anyone adding something to the tank which would ruin your engine.

Even your car wheels are worth money. A neighbour of mine recently had one of her car wheels stolen overnight. Next morning, she did not notice it was missing as it was an offside wheel and the thief had propped the car up on bricks. Her two children climbed in the back ready for the trip to school, she started the engine and was about to move off. Had another neighbour not shouted a warning just in time, she would certainly have done a good deal of damage to the car, and the children may have been hurt too. A set of four locking wheel nuts (i.e. one for each wheel) costs around £25.

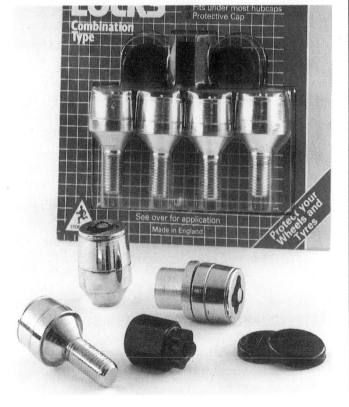

A pack of four locking wheel nuts – one for each wheel.

Thefts *of* cars

New or nearly new cars

If you own a new or fairly new car, it is likely to be most at risk from the professional car thief who will change the registration number plate, remove any identifying marks and sell the car as quickly as possible. Very often he will sell it abroad, particularly if it is an upmarket car like a Mercedes, Jaguar, Daimler, or one of the top-of-the-range BMW or Volkswagen models.

Prevention measures

● Whenever you leave your car, make sure all the windows, doors and the boot are locked and that the steering lock, if you have one, has been engaged.

● Park in a well-lit area whenever possible, and with your front wheels turned sharply towards the kerb to make it difficult for a thief to tow the car away.

● Have your registration number etched onto all the windows – preferably near the top of each one so that the thief cannot hide the marks by winding the windows down a little. This may deter a thief whose plan is to 'ring' the car, i.e. steal it, change the number plates to those of an insurance write-off or an old banger, and use its documents to give your car a whole new identity. If the windows have been etched, he'll realise that he will have to go to the trouble and expense of replacing all the glass, and possibly risk alerting the supplier's suspicions as well.

● Fit a car alarm (see pages 69–73), and preferably an immobiliser (a hidden switch in the ignition circuit) as well. An immobiliser switch will cost £10–12, but they are usually not too difficult for a determined thief to find, so I would not recommend relying on one without an alarm.

● Fit an internal locking device:

For about £20, you can buy an electronic lock which will not allow the engine to start until you have keyed the correct code into a touchpad fixed to the dashboard.

A combination lock is available which is attached to the handbrake, making it difficult for the thief to drive away. You can engage and disengage it by means of your own three-digit combination, and it costs about £14.

● There is also a lock (costing about £15) which fits over both the handbrake and the gear stick, making it impossible for the thief to get the car into gear or take the handbrake off.

This lock fits over the handbrake and locks around the gear lever.

Older cars

Cars which are more than 10 years old are several times more likely to be stolen than newer ones. They are usually easier to break into, more difficult to protect and less conspicuous. They are frequently taken by joyriders which means that although you are much more likely to get your car back, it will probably have been damaged. There is evidence that a high number of stolen cars are involved in accidents.

Prevention measures

● Make sure all the locks work and are not badly worn. You may need to buy and fit replacement locks.

● As well as locking up all round, double-check the quarterlight windows to make sure they are secure. This is still the most common means of breaking into older cars.

● Fit an immobiliser or combination lock (see pages 66 and 67).

● A steering wheel lock, such as a Krooklock at about £9, can be a good and inexpensive deterrent if your car does not have one built in.

A steering wheel lock should be fitted under the brake pedal.

Car alarms

As with house burglar alarms, just being able to see that an alarm has been installed is a very important deterrent to a car thief. It's the only effective way of halting a casual thief in his tracks. It will cost between £50 and £500, depending on how sophisticated the system is.

There is quite a wide range of alarms and anti-theft devices on the market now, and each make of car has different vulnerable points, so I'd recommend finding a reputable dealer (again, your Crime Prevention Officer will be able to help). A knowledgeable and trustworthy dealer can show you what is available and advise on what is best for your car, how much at risk from break-ins it might be and how much you might need to spend. Organisations like the AA or the RAC also offer free advice on security to their members.

Main types of alarm

Most of these alarms will need to be fitted by specialists:

Ignition cut-out

This is the simplest type of alarm and is designed to stop the car itself being stolen. It is usually linked to the car's horn and sounds a warning at the same time as blocking the ignition circuit. It is operated by a concealed switch or a key, and costs around £30.

Voltage drop

In this device (costing about £25) a sensor is wired into the car's electrical circuit, which detects a drop in the voltage – for example, it will trigger the alarm when the courtesy light comes on as the door is opened. This is also turned on or off with a switch or a key.

Pin-switch

The pin-switch is wired directly to the door. When the door is opened, the pin is released from the switch which earths the electrics and the alarm goes off. The device can be linked to an independent siren, which is much more difficult for a thief to find and disconnect than the car horn. Pin-switches can also be fitted to safeguard the boot, bonnet or any other point of entry, and will set you back about £2.50.

Pendulum

This type of alarm is set off when the car is rocked, jolted or moved in any way, and costs around £25. The 'pendulum' is a small weight on the end of a light spring with a contact underneath the weight. When something causes the spring to vibrate, the weight touches the contact and sounds the alarm. You can adjust their sensitivity, but nevertheless the disadvantage of this type is that they can sometimes be triggered too readily by the vibration of a passing bus or lorry, for example. Too many false alarms, especially during the night, can be exasperating not only for you, but for your neighbours as well. Even more important, people will stop taking the noise seriously.

Trembler switch

This device is similar to the pendulum alarm and has a ball bearing between two contacts. Any definite movement of the car – if someone tries to open a door, for example – causes the ball bearing to touch the contacts and trigger the alarm. A trembler switch should be available for about £25.

Ultrasonic

Ultrasonic detectors emit sound waves, and the siren is triggered if the frequency pattern of the sound waves is disturbed by someone trying to break in. The alarms are usually fitted on the parcel shelf behind the rear seats, and the system costs in the region of £50.

Passive

There is also the passive alarm system (costing about £47) which sets itself once you have locked the car. It allows you enough time to get into the car before the siren goes off, and is armed and disarmed by means of a concealed switch inside the car.

Infra-red

This system uses an infra-red transmitter that you keep on your key fob. You aim the device towards the receiver which is fitted inside the car, press a button and *Hey presto*!, it locks all the doors and sets the alarm. With some systems of this type, the car even dutifully flashes its headlights to indicate message received and understood! You switch it off and un-lock the doors in the same way. This type of alarm will cost around £45.

Extras

● A light-flashing facility can be wired into any of the above alarm systems as a supplement to the siren, and will add about £5 to the cost.

● Panic buttons (about £5 each) can be fitted to any alarm system (but preferably one which operates the central locking device), usually in a strategic place inside the car, as a safeguard against personal attack. These are particularly useful for people who have to carry high-risk goods in the course of their job, or to the drivers of large commercial vehicles who sleep in their lorries at night.

● Roof racks and trailers can be fitted with a remote sensor alarm, available for around £5.

You can 'mix and match' as many of these features as you like or can afford.

Many car alarm systems are powered by the car's own battery, although you can fit a second power unit by way of back-up. This increases reliability but is really only essential in vehicles like a lot of commercial ones, where it is easy to gain access to the battery terminals in order to disconnect the alarm, or if you carry high-risk items around in your car as part of your business. Even with the battery locked away under the bonnet, a determined thief would still be able to disconnect the wiring from underneath the car, so a back-up power facility could be worth considering.

For the most reliable security and the greatest peace of mind, it is worth paying extra for an alarm to be installed by specialists who can fit infra-red monitoring and closed circuit wiring and who offer good after-sales service. Closed circuit wiring means your alarm will sound even if the wires are tampered with.

DIY car alarms

If you feel a simpler system is adequate to protect your car and you want to fit your own, there are several kits on the market to choose from. Most DIY alarms use the voltage drop method but in case the courtesy light stops working for some reason, it is best to supplement this either with pin-switches on all possible entry points, or with an ultrasonic detector unit. (All are described on pages 69–71.)

Most of the basic kits are designed to use the car horn as the sounder, but you would be much better advised to fit a siren powered by a separate battery. This is partly to avoid the risk of running the car battery down, and partly so that it is obvious to anyone who hears it that it is an alarm and not someone leaning on the car horn for some reason! Sirens are available from £18.

Choose a system which cuts out automatically after five minutes and then re-sets – most of them do anyway. Most kits also include an ignition cut-out which automatically immobilises the car when the alarm is triggered, or you could buy an engine immobiliser and fit it with an alarm. You may want to choose a system which is flexible enough to allow you to add any extra features you might want in the future.

The more expensive kits are often simpler to install, with fewer wires to connect and fewer holes to drill. Some kits require no wires at all. One system simply consists of a keypad, which you fit to the dashboard and activate by entering your personal code, and a vibration sensor to trigger the siren.

Whatever alarm you choose, if it's to do its job it must be fitted properly. Make sure you have the right tools for the job before you start and read the instructions carefully! If you have any doubts about doing the job yourself, ask an expert.

Whether you fit a simple alarm system yourself or opt for a more sophisticated professionally installed one, it is most important that your system does not give out frequent false alarms. In the past this was such a problem with certain types of car alarm that we all became rather complacent about the sound of an alarm going off. Since 1981 it's been illegal for car alarms to sound for longer than five minutes. Now all installers fit alarm systems with this limitation as standard. Because of this, the noise your alarm makes should be as penetrating as possible to be really effective.

Your alarm system should also be checked regularly to make sure it is in good working order – most dealers recommend a service every eight months or so. Finally, whatever type of system you have, remember that the deterrent value alone is very important. Make the fact that your car has an alarm as obvious as possible.

Parking safely

Where you choose to park is an important factor in preventing theft from or of your car. Try to pick a well-lit area rather than a dark side street where a thief can work unobserved. If you park in daylight, think ahead about whether it will still be light by the time you return. If not, choose a place where there are street lights and for your own safety, don't park in a place where you will have to walk back to the car through unlit alleys or subways. It is worth being late for an appointment to make sure you find a better parking place.

In multi-storey car parks, park as near as you can to the entrance where the ticket office and parking attendants are. If possible, it is better to park in the busiest part and avoid the upper floors so that you are less remote and there are fewer of those unpleasant concrete staircases to negotiate. Keep the car park ticket with you – don't leave it inside the car so that a thief can easily drive out.

Bear in mind that if you use a 'Pay and display' car park, the ticket on your dashboard will tell a thief how long you intend to be away from the car.

Pay and display car parks – they're very easy. I know a car park where you can guarantee there's as many as 200 cars overnight. It's easy pickings. They've got street lights on in the car parks but it's still easy.

Be alert. It makes sense to be practical and on your guard without being paranoid and terrified that you are going to be raped or murdered at any moment. All the same, if you can avoid subways, dark stairways or lifts at night it's obviously better to do so. If there is going to be any danger to yourself, the most likely moment is when you are standing next to the car, fumbling for your keys.

If ever you think something may be wrong, don't get into your car, but retrace your steps as quickly as you can to a lighted area where there are people around, and explain your suspicions to someone.

If you are parking in an open car park, it is always better to park in the middle, rather than round the edge where there may be trees or other places where a thief could lurk and break into your car under cover of darkness.

A car thief says:
It's easy to deal with those hook-type steering locks – the ones which hook over the steering wheel and the clutch pedal. All you do is stamp hard down on the clutch. The steering wheel bends quite easily and the lock comes off. People would be better advised to use the brake pedal with those locks, because it can't be 'floored' so easily.

The built-in steering locks which you engage when you turn the ignition off aren't too much of a problem if I really fancy a particular motor. I've got a couple of ways of dealing with them. I've got one special tool which pulls the guts out of the lock, and one which clamps onto the steering column and sheers off the lock pins.

Basically, what one man can invent, another man can get round. I must admit though that a car alarm is a bit of a turn-off. You have to take the time factor into account. If I see someone leaving their motor and going into a cinema, for example, then obviously I know I've got plenty of leeway. Parking meters and those 'Pay and display' car park tickets people have to leave on their windscreens are a great guide to how long the owner is going to be away.

Protecting your caravan

Start by safeguarding the caravan itself by making sure it cannot be towed away. The first thing a thief will look at is the towbar. If it is not locked into a cover, he can easily hitch it to his own vehicle and tow the caravan away. The best and simplest deterrent is a hitchlock. There are several different types on the market, but if you choose one that needs a padlock, get a close shackle one. Open shackle padlocks are easy to cut through (see page 32).

Padlocks can also be used to stop the would-be thief from raising the corner legs, or you can buy special clamps to lock each leg firmly into position. The wheels can be vulnerable too, so fit these with locking wheel nuts in the same way as you would on a car (see page 65). If you are not planning to move the caravan for some time, you can jack it up and remove one of the wheels, or invest in a wheel clamp to prevent anyone towing it away.

Etch the windows with your chassis number or registration number but *not* your postcode. When you are away on holiday with the caravan, you could be directing a thief straight to your house, which he will now know is likely to be unoccupied! Also, if your caravan is normally outside your house all year round and it suddenly disappears for two weeks, then anyone up to no good can be fairly sure that the

This towball is inserted into the ball socket of your caravan or trailer. It can only be removed by using the correct key bar.

house-breaking prospects are bright. This is when
belonging to a Neighbourhood Watch scheme (see
page 45), having marked property and good all-round
security really come into their own.

Thefts *from* caravans

Stealing *from* caravans is usually the work of our old
friend the opportunist casual thief, who is likely to be
deterred quite easily if you just make things difficult
for him. So your caravan should be protected in much
the same way as your home is. Keep the caravan
securely locked all the time, even if it is parked right
outside your house or in your driveway. You will
probably need to supplement all the manufacturer's
locks with stronger ones of your own – the door
should have a good secure mortise deadlock (see
page 9) or a padbar and close shackle padlock (see
page 32). Always close and lock all the windows,
doors and sun roof when you leave the caravan, even
if it is only for a few minutes.

Close the curtains so that thieves can't see if you
have anything worth stealing. Items that may be a
target, such as a radio, TV set, portable cooker and so
on, should be property marked (see page 36) and
stickers displayed in the windows to advertise the
fact. Again, I would advise using your car registration
number rather than your postcode to mark them.

Outside the caravan, the gas cylinders are particularly vulnerable to passing thieves. These should be
chained and padlocked (again using a close shackle
padlock) to the fixing clamps which keep them up-
right or to the towbar frame. If they are kept in a
special container on the towbar frame, make sure
that it is always locked.

There are now small alarm systems available
which have been especially designed for caravans.
These are either electronic or battery-powered and
are usually quite simple to fit yourself. DIY kits include a control unit, a bell or siren box, an anti-tilt or

movement detector, a junction box and the necessary wire, and cost between £45 and £90. Some makes have rechargeable batteries, others run off your car battery (so that you can only use them when you are on the road touring) or on mains electricity which can only be used on caravan sites which have their own power supply. Make sure the siren or bell is weatherproof and not easily sabotaged. At night, if you are away for the evening, leave a light on inside the caravan so that it looks as though people are inside. It's cheap and easy to put a light on a timer switch (see page 31).

If you are staying on a caravan site, it's a good idea to set up a kind of Neighbourhood Watch, so that everyone can keep an eye out for anything suspicious. Don't forget, however, that caravans kept permanently on a site are especially vulnerable in winter when most of them are unoccupied, so that is when all these security measures are particularly important. If you are going to leave your caravan empty and unattended for some time, whether on a site or in your driveway, take everything of any value out, leave the empty drawers open, and draw back the curtains so that prying eyes can see there is nothing worth breaking in for.

Protecting your boat

When your boat is at home, it should be permanently chained and padlocked to the trailer and kept out of sight in a locked garage if possible. Keep the trailer from being towed away by chaining it to an immovable fixture like a concrete post, or by immobilising it with a wheel clamp or a hitchlock (see page 76).

The most stealable – and stealworthy – item on a boat is probably the outboard motor, which is quite easy and quick to remove. So keep it secured at all times with an anti-theft device, whether the boat is on the water or in transit on the road. Chain and lock or bolt it in place and obscure the securing nuts with a good strong padlock.

If you leave the boat at its moorings for more than a day or two, take the motor with you, locked in the boot of your car. Obviously while your boat is at home, you will keep the motor safely indoors. Etch or die-stamp a security code on it – *not* your postcode, as this could inform a thief of your address while you are away (see page 36 on property marking). Use a security code of your own – your car registration number, for example. Keep a note of the make, model and serial number, and if you have a radio on board, make a note of the serial number of that too. At least then you have some chance of recovering it if it is stolen.

All valuables which can be locked away out of sight should be kept in a strong locker with a good lock on it. Main doors and hatches should be secured with a mortise deadlock and all windows closed and locked.

When you land, mooring with just ropes is not secure enough. Chain the boat to a ring, and padlock the chain with a close shackle, weatherproof padlock (see page 32).

If your boat has a dinghy or other smaller boat attached, mark it with the main vessel's name and your security code. Surfboards, canoes or inflatable dinghies and so on should be marked in the same way, and chain and lock them to the car roof rack when you are on the road. The more valuable your boat is, the more worthwhile it is investing in an alarm to protect it. The alarm will have to be one that isn't triggered too easily by wind or tide. You can get good advice on this from reputable boat dealers, security firms, insurance companies and, of course, the Crime Prevention Officer at your local police headquarters.

Finally, if you are holidaying at a marina, it is worth forming a sort of temporary 'Neighbourhood Watch' so that you can all keep an eye on each other's boats. A good marina should have its own security guard.

Protecting your bicycle

Living in London as I do, I have heard it said that if you can keep a bike for more than five years you deserve an entry in *The Guinness Book of Records*! It is certainly true that in some areas the number of bike thefts is increasing, and only about 4 per cent of stolen bikes are ever reunited with their owners. Expensive modern machines like mountain bikes, touring bikes and racers are big business to thieves, and some are not above pinching an old push-bike, or your child's bike either.

Leaving your bike unlocked at any time, even for a few moments while you call in quickly at a shop, is risky. Most bicycles are stolen on the spur of the moment. You should always lock your bike, even if you think you're parking it on safe ground, like the stairwell of a block of flats. Locking helps but it can still be at risk, so try to park in a busy, well-lit place where there are plenty of passers-by. If you regularly park your bike in the same place for the same length of time – for example, if you use it to travel to and from work, it won't be too difficult for someone to plot exactly how and when he can steal it. Ask your employer to provide secure parking. If this is not possible, then you will have to rely on using the best lock you can. At home, keep your bike chained to a secure fixture in a locked building or garage.

Bicycle locks

Cycle locks range in price from about £10 to £25. If you spend less than that, you really will not be buying a very effective one. The most expensive ones are the very heavy rigid U-shaped locks, such as Kryptonite and Citadel, or the No-Crak lock and chain. The manufacturers claim that these can resist the most formidable of cutting tools, and most of them include free insurance. Look carefully at the small print though – there are usually some pretty stringent conditions!

A rigid U-shaped bike lock.

Loop a chain through the frame *and* wheel of your bike (preferably both wheels if the chain is long enough).

Alternatively, you could opt for a heavy-duty, case-hardened chain and a good-quality padlock. A close shackle padlock is best, although more expensive (see page 32). Always make sure you are buying hardened steel products. Avoid wire rope locks – these are too easily dealt with by a thief.

Thread the chain through the frame *and* the wheel or, preferably, *both* wheels if you buy a long enough chain – especially if you have 'quick-release' wheels. Loop it round something solid and immovable, like a lamp post. It is not much use just locking the front wheel; you're likely to come back and find the wheel still there, chained where you left it, but the rest of your bike gone! And make sure the object you lock your bike to really *is* immoveable. I have heard of someone chaining their bike to some railings, only to find bike, railings and all had vanished when he returned! Someone else who chained his bike to a traffic sign came back to find only a pole. The sign had been removed and the bike and chain lifted up and over the top of the pole.

Accessories

Accessories such as lamps, pumps, panniers, saddles, gears – even brakes and wheels – are common targets for thieves too. The advice here is to take what you can with you when you leave the bike, and what you can't take with you, bolt on as securely as you can. I know people who go so far as to take the front wheel away with them every time they park the bike. As long as it has the lightweight quick-release type of wheels, this is a relatively easy and effective measure.

Marking

Have the frame stamped with your postcode. This has the double advantage of acting as a deterrent to thieves and increasing the likelihood of getting the bike back if it *is* stolen. Good cycle shops now have stamping equipment, and many police stations offer this service if you take the bike there. Ask them for a 'cycle coded' sticker too; that in itself adds to the deterrent effect. As an extra precaution, keep a luggage label with your name and address on it hidden underneath the saddle. You are also more likely to get your bike back if you have kept a note of the exact make and model, the frame size and frame number, the number of gears, colour, type of handlebars and any other distinguishing features. By the way, the more distinctive you can make your bike look the better.

Insuring your bike

The cheapest way of insuring your bike is to add it to your household contents policy, but as always with insurance policies, it's important to study the small print carefully. Some policies limit the amount they will pay out on a stolen bicycle to £100 or less. For some extraordinary reason, some companies even charge extra on your cycle premium if you live with people to whom you are not related! Many policies do not include any third party insurance either, in which case you will not be covered if you cause any damage or injury whilst riding your bike.

Most of the bigger cycle shops can arrange theft insurance for you, or you could join one of the specialist cycling organisations which offer all kinds of support and advantages, including insurance policies at favourable rates. Local cycle dealers or public libraries will give you the name of your nearest organisation. If you live in London, the London Cycling Campaign is at 3 Stamford Street, London SE1 9NT.

Protecting your motorcycle

It is usually joyriders who steal motorcycles, only to abandon them later when the fun is over. The bigger, expensive, 'exotic' bikes are more likely to be stolen to be sold to lucrative markets either here or abroad. To protect your bike from theft one of the most important factors is where you park it. The same rules apply as those for parking cars (see pages 74–5). Leave it somewhere well lit and well populated and chain it to a fixed object, like a lamp post, with a good solid lock and chain. Most reputable motorcycle dealers will advise on the best kind of lock to buy. When your bike is at home, it is better to lock it away in a shed or garage, if possible, rather than keep it in the road, and in any case, don't leave it parked out on the street in the same place for days on end.

You can fit an immobiliser switch and an alarm to your bike. Alarms are rather vulnerable on motorbikes because they are relatively easy to get at, but they will probably deter the opportunist thief.

One very important point is *never* to leave your crash helmet with the bike – not even if it is locked away in the top box or chained to the handlebars. A thief will not want to attract police attention by breaking the law riding a bike without wearing a crash helmet. If the helmet is locked to the handlebars though, he could still come up with a plausible story about losing the key!

So, to sum up, keep your bike safe by parking it in a sensible place; locking it up when you leave it; never leaving the crash helmet with it; and not leaving anything of value in the panniers or top box.

Section 3

Personal safety

In this section I've given advice and some stories about how other people have coped in various circumstances, but, of course, it's all very well to theorise. In practice, if you should ever find yourself in a potentially dangerous situation, your own instincts will always be your best guide.

Keeping yourself safe

Rule number one in keeping yourself safe is to try to look like a strong-minded and confident person, whether you are walking along the street, sitting on a bus or driving your car. Body language is very important indeed, and studies have shown that someone who looks nervous, vague or insecure is far more likely to be the victim of an attack than someone who looks purposeful and determined. Many attackers expect their victims to be frightened of them – in fact the enjoyment of their sense of power is sometimes often largely why they attack people in the first place.

A confident manner can help you to cope with a threatening situation too. Attackers might expect you to shiver, shake and plead, so calm confidence may throw them off-balance. If you can look an attacker in the eye and say something like, 'Listen, just take your hands off me and get out of here NOW,' sounding firm, strong and genuinely angry, there is a good chance that he will simply go away.

How do you achieve this confidence? To a large extent it comes simply from being prepared, mentally and physically – and *knowing* that you're prepared. That means firstly not putting yourself in situations where you're obviously at risk, and secondly, having thought out what you would do if someone did attack you.

You don't need to curtail your own freedom unduly, or constantly expect the worst to happen. You just need to be alert and sensible and use a little forethought.

❜ *It's my job to visit people in their own homes and sometimes this means I have to travel up in the lifts. I used to be really scared of being trapped by someone so I've got lots of little tricks now.*

Sometimes if the lift comes and I don't like the look of the person I pretend I've forgotten something and just walk away till the doors close and I can get the next one. When I'm in the lift I usually start up conversations about the weather or the state of the lifts. I try and put things on an ordinary chatty basis because I think then it's harder for someone to turn into an attacker. I stand by the buttons so it's me that says 'What floor?' If I don't feel happy I say 'Oh, I pressed the wrong number, it's this floor I want' and I get out. ❜

When you go out, think ahead about where you are going and how you will get there and back. If you are likely to be leaving somewhere alone, late at night, arrange to be met at the station or bus stop, or book a taxi or minicab – preferably in advance – through a licensed firm you trust. When you get home, you could ask the driver to wait until you are safely inside. Have your house keys ready so that you are not standing on the doorstep, fumbling around looking for them. Whenever possible, organise yourself a lift from someone you know – but make sure you really do know them:

❜ *I went to a friend's party and it was really late but this man who I know from our office was there and he said he'd give me a lift home. Of course I just said yes. I mean, I knew him and I*

87

didn't think anything would happen.

Anyway he started saying how he really liked me and I just felt embarrassed to begin with but then noticed that he wasn't going towards my house but back out of the town. For a while I felt scared. I thought 'Oh my God, this is actually happening to me!' But then I thought 'Why should he do this? Who does he think he is?' I said, 'Listen, I thought you said you'd take me straight home.' He was horrible, he said some horrible things about me and then tried to turn it all into a joke. I just kept saying 'Take me home right now. You said you'd take me home.' In the end he turned round and drove me back. When I got to my road he said he wasn't really going to do anything. I think he was scared then that I'd tell everyone at work. Too right – I did! 🔊

On foot

Try to avoid being out and about alone, late at night, if you can possibly help it. It is most unusual for people in groups of two or more to be attacked. But if you have to be out alone, avoid dimly lit areas and back streets if you can, even if it means walking further.

Keep to the centre of the pavement, away from bushes or dark buildings. Women who go out some-where special for the evening, wearing their best high heels, should perhaps think about taking a com-fortable flat pair to change into afterwards. Not only are they much more comfortable, but they are much easier to run in if you should need to get away fast from an unpleasant situation.

It is a good idea to have a torch with you, and walk facing the oncoming traffic. Unless there's a *real* emergency, *never* hitch or accept a lift from strang-ers, no matter how tempting it may be to get out of the rain or rest your aching feet. If someone stops to ask you for directions, keep far enough away from the car not to be grabbed and pulled inside.

One of the most unnerving experiences is being followed late at night. If this happens to you, you could try crossing the street a few times. If that doesn't shake him off, hurry towards an area where you know there will be lights and people, or go to the nearest occupied house. If someone follows you in a car, try turning round and walking briskly in the opposite direction. It will be difficult for him to turn the car round quickly. And if all your instincts tell you he's not going to be deterred – *run*. Again, head for people and lights, or seek help at a nearby house. Try to take note of the registration number and make of the car.

This man got off the bus and I just knew he was following me. I felt quite panicky but I crossed over the road and slowed down and I managed to get behind him. It was funny then because I made him *feel scared and he rushed off.*

It's easy to look like rich pickings for a mugger without realising it. Think carefully before walking along the street obviously wearing valuable jewellery. It's best either to leave it at home, or keep it covered up.

Foiling pickpockets and bagsnatchers

Pickpockets often work in teams of two or three. First of all, one of them jostles you – you pat your wallet pocket or check your bag to make sure your money is still there. It is, so you relax; but the thieves now know exactly what they are aiming for! While one bumps into you to distract your attention, another snatches your wallet.

Bagsnatching is usually done 'on the run'. The thief grabs the strap of your bag as he rushes past you, taking you completely by surprise. This is usually an opportunist crime – so don't provide the opportunity. To foil bagsnatchers, hold the bag tightly under your arm or in front of you, and have the strap across your

Wear your handbag across you body. If it has lots of compartments keep them all tightly zipped up. If possible, hold the bag firmly in front of you.

chest so it can't easily be grasped from behind.

Don't carry large sums of cash around with you, and keep your cheque book and cheque card in separate places, so that if someone does steal your bag they cannot use your cheque book. And if you must carry large sums around, at least divide the money up between several pockets in order to make things harder for the thief.

One clever trick is to wear a small, flat shoulder bag across your chest, *under* your coat, and use it to carry most of your money, your cheque card and anything else of particular value. In the second handbag, worn *outside* your coat, keep your cheque book, the small change you need for fares and payphones, and the rest of the paraphernalia you usually carry. That way if you fall victim to a bag-snatcher or pickpocket, he'll get away with very little. Ideally handbags should have a flap covering zipped-up compartments with a good secure fastener.

Briefcases or cameras worn over the shoulder are vulnerable in the same way as handbags. You can now buy special security briefcases which have built-in alarms designed to go off when the case is separated from its owner. If someone does try to take your bag or case, remember that, in the end, it is better to let him have it than risk personal injury by trying to protect it.

Rather than carry your house and car keys in your bag, put them in your pocket or wherever you can reach them easily and quickly. And to avoid receiving a visit from a burglar, never keep your house keys in the same place as any papers which have your name and address on them.

Something else you should not carry in your handbag is a personal alarm if you have one. There is little point in having an alarm if it isn't readily to hand within seconds (see page 100).

On public transport

When you are using public transport, try not to wait at deserted bus stops, and on the bus, stick to the lower deck nearer the driver and conductor. As for travelling on the train (both Underground and British Rail), British Transport Police give the following advice:

● Try not to wait at lonely, unmanned stations. If possible, either plan ahead to avoid this, or ask the person who takes you to the station to see you on to the train.

● Try to avoid travelling alone late at night.

● When the train arrives, look for a compartment with male and female passengers, and try not to get into one of those carriages with neither corridors nor interconnecting doors. British Rail are phasing them out, I'm glad to say.

● If someone does pester you, change compartments using the interconnecting doors.

The official advice about pulling the communication cord is that you should only do so 'if you are in fear of your life'. I would imagine, however, that by the time that happens, you are unlikely to be in a position to reach it! My personal advice is that if you do feel seriously threatened, use the cord. Your safety is more important than disrupting schedules or risking a £50 fine.

91

In your car

If you are out in your own car at night, it goes without saying that you should make sure you have enough petrol to get there and back – and keep a full petrol can in the boot, just in case.

I will never forget one tragic case we reconstructed on *Crimewatch* in 1985. A young woman had a job working a couple of evenings a week at a pub, saving up to get married. One night after finishing her stint, she left for home as usual in her van, but ran out of petrol on the way. She was last seen alive at around midnight, carrying her empty petrol can in the direction of the nearest petrol station. If only she hadn't let her tank get so low . . . if only her spare can had been full . . . then no one would have had an opportunity to attack her that night.

It makes sense to keep your car regularly serviced and in good running order, and not to set out alone in your car at night, knowing that it is likely to break down. If you *are* unlucky enough to break down or have a puncture late at night, even if you think you can fix whatever is wrong yourself, it is safer to call someone else for assistance.

I would recommend joining one of the motoring organisations like the AA or the RAC, and always keep some change in the glove compartment for the phone and perhaps carry a phone card too. Whoever you call for help, wait safely in your car until that help arrives. If there is no public phone nearby, police advise you to wait in your locked car – all night if necessary, or until someone waiting for you to come home alerts the police, or until you can flag down a passing police car. Before setting out on any journey, particularly late at night, it's worth making sure that someone knows when and where you're going and perhaps even arranging to phone them when you arrive safely – just in case anything goes wrong.

If a stranger offers help, use your instincts to

decide whether or not he (or she) is trustworthy, but err on the distrustful side if you have any doubts at all. Don't offer lifts to strangers or to hitch-hikers. The most helpful course of action if you see someone in trouble is to drive on quickly to the nearest phone box or police station and report it.

If ever you are followed in your car by another motorist, as has happened to two of my women friends late at night, keep cool. Don't drive home, but head for the nearest busy lit-up area, and look for a police station. On both occasions, when my friends stopped at the blue lamp, the man quickly drove away, and in one of the cases, the pursuer turned out to be someone the police had been looking for in connection with serious sexual offences. So try to make a note of the pursuer's registration number.

If you are followed home in your car and can't easily get to a police station for some reason, don't get out, but lock yourself in, hoot and flash your lights, which will attract attention and almost certainly frighten the man off pretty quickly.

If you see what looks like an accident late at night in a place where there are no other people about, think twice before you stop to offer assistance. This may sound hard-hearted, but it just could be a trap, and actually, unless you are a qualified nurse or doctor, or have been taught to give emergency aid there isn't likely to be much you could do anyway. Again, the best course of action is to drive on and report it.

If, however, you see someone fighting off what could be an attacker or if ever you hear screaming, don't just shrug it off as a domestic argument which is 'none of your business' or as young people playing around. It is quite probable that someone needs help. Preserve your own safety; you don't have to get involved in any fight or argument yourself, but get to the nearest phone and call the police at once.

There have been several cases on *Crimewatch* where neighbours have turned a deaf ear to screams or noises in the night, having convinced themselves that it was probably nothing serious and that they shouldn't get involved. The result was serious injury or, on more than one occasion, a murder which might have been prevented by one simple phone call to the police. The police would much prefer you to call them out in error rather than not call them at all and let a crime happen.

Parking safely

When you are parking your car, think ahead to whether you are likely to be coming back to the car after dark and make sure you have parked it somewhere busy and well lit, not where you will have to walk through dark back streets to find it. It is worth being late for an appointment to make sure you find a better parking place.

In multi-storey car parks, park as near as you can to the entrance where the attendants are. Ideally, it is best to park in the busiest part and avoid the upper floors so that you are less remote, and there are fewer of those unpleasant concrete staircases to negotiate. It's obviously safer to avoid subways, dark stairways or lifts at night if you can.

If you are parking in an open car park, it is always safer to park in the middle of it rather than near the edge, where someone could be lurking under cover of trees, bushes or fences.

If there is going to be any danger to yourself, the most likely moment is when you are standing next to the car fumbling for your keys, so make sure you have them ready before you get there. Before you open the car door, take a routine look inside, and if you think something may be wrong, don't get in. Instead, retrace your steps as quickly as you can to the lighted area where there are people around, and explain your suspicions to someone.

Once you've got into your car, lock the door until you've driven off. You may, in any case, feel safer to keep all the doors locked whilst driving slowly through built-up areas (but don't forget to unlock them again when you're on the open road in case of an accident).

Flashers

I heard this man say 'Come and have a look at this.' I was walking past the park at the time. He looked quite respectable to me and I started going towards him. Then, of course, I realised what was going on, felt frightened and ran. I did phone up and report it. People think flashers are funny but it's horrible when they pick on you. I had to remember that there was nothing wrong with me.

At some time in their lives many women will have encountered a flasher – a man who exposes himself in public. Younger women can probably laugh it off more easily than older women, but it is important to try not to show the flasher any feelings of shock or disgust, as this is exactly what he wants and expects. If possible, the best course of action is to ignore him completely.

A man exposed himself to me on a London tube train a few years ago and asked me what I thought of the prized part of his anatomy. Instinctively I thought the best move would be to provide an excuse for his behaviour which he could use as a way out. I glanced indifferently at what he was showing me, then looked him in the eye and asked if he was drunk. To my relief, it worked. His swaggering bravado crumbled. He just said 'Yes I am', and as the train pulled into the next station, turned and got out, still fastening his trousers and looking very sheepish.

Most flashers are sad, inadequate characters rather than a real threat to society, but since they can be very upsetting, and since they do sometimes become dangerous, it's best to report an incident like this to the police.

Self-defence

In writing this book I have quite deliberately chosen not to illustrate how to get out of a half-nelson in elaborate detail or 20 different ways of trying to im-mobilise an attacker. This is because a little knowl-edge of self-defence can be far more dangerous than no knowledge at all. If you are going to attempt any self-defence moves against someone who attacks you, then you have to make sure it is going to work.

One self-defence strategem worth knowing: stamp hard down your attacker's shin and on to his foot with as much force as you can muster.

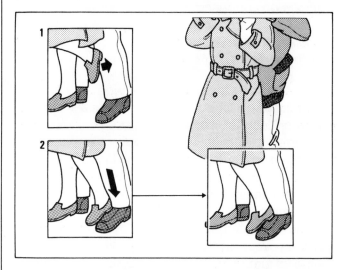

Otherwise, you will not only have failed to deter your attacker, but you may have increased his anger and aggression into the bargain, leaving you in a more dangerous situation than you were before.

The only tactic I think is worth mentioning here is a hard kick on the shins – administered with as much strength and anger as you can muster, suddenly and without warning. It is very painful, and an attacker will feel shocked and sick for a few seconds – enough to give you a chance to get away. If you are attacked from behind, stamp on the inside of the attacker's foot as hard as you can, scraping your shoe down his shin as you do so – that will have a similar effect. Don't let him see you thinking about it, just do it – *immediately*. Shouting very loudly at the same time will have even more impact. It's good to be angry; it'll help you feel stronger and less frightened – 'How *dare* he do this to you!'

❙ *I was walking down the road and my bag was grabbed by this man. I didn't think. I was just so angry. I had my pay and I was on my way to buy my little girl's birthday present. I stood there and shouted at him. I wouldn't let go. It was all so quick but I must have looked so determined he realised it wasn't worth the battle. I was just so angry. I'd worked for that money. Why should he get it?* **❚**

The problem with self-defence is that it is very difficult for most women to bring themselves to really hurt someone. A common suggestion is to poke your middle and index fingers hard into an attacker's eyes, but in reality few women could do that with the viciousness needed to do enough damage to put him out of action.

If you think you *could* carry out moves like this with real force, then I strongly advise going to a proper course of self-defence classes. Your local council education authority, public library or sports centre will usually have details of courses where you live. If possible, go to classes which are either run by the police or recommended by them. Both the qualifications and motives of some commercial instructors are highly dubious. In the Greater London area the police can provide qualified instructors who will run four-week courses for organised groups of women who want to learn self-defence and can provide the premises. They are suitable for all ages and levels of fitness. For details, write to: The Metropolitan Special Constabulary, A6 Branch (SD), New Scotland Yard, Broadway, London SW1H 0BG.

If a course in self-defence makes you feel more confident, then that in itself is well worth it. Personally, I believe that going to fitness classes can be just as effective, so that you are in good condition to choose the first and most obvious option if you are approached by someone who seems to want to harm you – that is to *run* to where there are lights and people about. *Don't* risk staying and attempting to fight when there's a chance of getting away.

Having said that, physical fitness isn't everything either. Use your instincts. Many women have been able to talk their way out of a difficult situation, feigning a confidence that is far from what they feel.

Good self-defence can be anything that fits the circumstances you find yourself in. This might range from whacking your assailant over the head with a frozen chicken to embarking on the story of your life. You might even try singing:

❛ *I was walking back through my estate and for some reason started singing to myself. It was 'Moon River, wider than a mile'! It's not a song I even like. I was walking along and I was getting louder and louder. In fact I remember thinking 'Why are you being so noisy?' But I couldn't stop. I did notice these two young men standing near the block next to mine but I wasn't really conscious of danger although I didn't feel quite right. Anyway I got indoors, still singing, and forgot about it. Twenty minutes later my neighbour knocked at my door. She'd had her bag stolen by two blokes who were obviously the same two. Then, of course, I remembered about my singing. Somehow I had defended myself without realising it. The singing made me look confident so they had let me go.* ❜

Ideally, you will plan what to do beforehand. But if you're taken by surprise, only you can decide whether to run, talk or fight back.

Where you stand legally

You are entitled in law to use 'reasonable force' in order to prevent a crime or defend yourself – the force has to be in proportion to the threat. For example, if someone is abusing you verbally, you have no right to attack them physically. Reasonable force can include kicking, scratching, biting and as much physical force as you are capable of, depending on the circumstances. It can also include using keys to scratch or stab at an assailant, an umbrella or walking stick, hairspray (if you can get at it in time, which might be difficult) or anything else which you would be carrying for a perfectly legitimate reason. But what are *not* legitimate are knives, or anything else which could be described as an offensive weapon.

Knives and guns

As I have said before, an air of confidence comes largely from having thought about how you might react in a threatening situation, so it is worth working out what you would do if you did ever encounter someone armed with a knife or a gun.

Firstly, it is vital to keep your wits about you. There is no physical way you can match either a gun or a knife. In a situation like this, your best assets are your brain and your instincts; use them to try to talk your way out of danger. This may seem a tall order when you're likely to be terrified, but that's why it's such a good idea to think out in advance what you could do if you were ever in this situation. Deep breathing can help you cope with fear, and there are women's groups that offer support and the opportunity to try to prepare yourself for such an event (see pages 115–6). The more calm and reasonable you appear,

99

the less likely you are to provoke him into using the knife or gun, and the more likely he is to relax a little.

Then, wait and watch for anything that might distract his attention for a few moments, and seize the opportunity to run if you can. Do what he tells you to do; be aware of where the weapon is at all times, and don't make any sudden moves. Police advise that it is pointless to try to knock the weapon out of his hand unless you really feel it is your only chance of survival.

Personal alarms

If you often have to travel alone at night, it may be worth carrying a personal alarm, as long as you don't assume that carrying one means you will be able to deal with any kind of attack. There is one important caution to stress, however, and that is to think before using it if you are attacked in a remote area where no one is likely to hear it. You may simply make your attacker more aggressive for no useful purpose.

There are various kinds of alarm, but they all operate on the same principle – that is to make a painfully loud, high-pitched screeching noise designed to take your attacker by surprise and, hopefully, make him run off in the fear that someone will hear it and come to your assistance.

Some alarms are activated by compressed air, like an aerosol, and some are powered by a battery or a rechargeable power unit. Check it regularly, and if possible buy one which has an indicator light to tell you when the power is running low. The types of alarm which are operated by pressing a button or squeezing a trigger have the disadvantage that you have to keep pressing to keep them sounding, which may hamper your ability to fight back if you need to. However the type which works rather like a grenade, with a pin which you pull out to start the alarm, leaves your hands free because the noise continues until you switch it off or the power runs out.

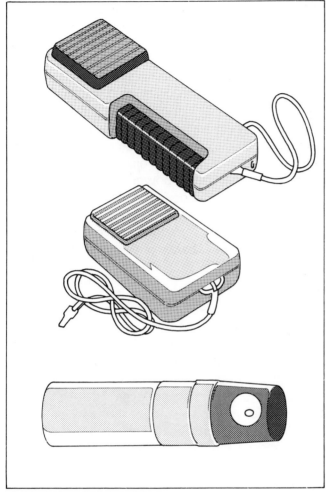

Three types of personal alarm: (top) this one has to be squeezed for the siren to sound; (centre) a 'grenade' type activated when the pin is pulled out; (bottom) an 'aerosol' type where you have to press down the top. Look for the kind that then locks into position so that the noise keeps going even when the alarm is dropped.

A whistle, sometimes called a 'rape whistle', is another means of surprising an attacker, although you should make sure it is loud enough to attract attention and it is better not to wear it round your neck.

Nuisance telephone callers

Men who find it exciting to make obscene telephone calls to women are very similar characters to flashers. Usually they are harmless – perhaps living in a fantasy world because, where relationships with women are concerned, they do not have the courage or confidence to live in the real one.

For the obscene phone caller, as with the flasher, the thrill comes from the reaction of fear and shock he hears in the woman's voice. It gives him the feeling of dominance and power he needs but cannot command with someone face to face. The owner of the voice which fills you with dread down the telephone may well be a mousy, conventional-looking man who you would hardly notice in the street.

What you can say

If you do find yourself on the receiving end of an obscene phone call, or a series of them, try to sound very matter of fact and rather contemptuous. Pretend you don't understand why he has called or what he is talking about, and suggest that perhaps he should talk to your husband (even if you don't have one!). Some women have found it effective to outdo the caller in the obscenity stakes, but the police advise against taunting or laughing at him, as this may push him into aggressive or even violent behaviour.

The advice from the police and British Telecom in dealing with what they call nuisance callers, is not to give them the satisfaction of entering into a dialogue at all, but just to hang up gently without saying anything – then they will probably give up through sheer boredom. You could try keeping a whistle by the phone to blow down the mouthpiece – that very often puts a stop to unwanted calls!

Why me?

Sometimes a caller will have found your number in the phone book. He will look particularly for women's first names, or where the listing quotes Miss, Ms or Mrs. So make sure that only your surname and initials are given in the book, or go ex-directory.

Some calls are hoaxes – often from children who perhaps think your name is amusing or are simply phoning to 'wind someone up'. Sometimes the caller will have dialled a number at random just to listen and see what the reaction is. Remember, though, that a silent call is often nothing more than a wrong number, and whoever it is may be too rude or embarrassed to apologise for it.

To be on the safe side, don't give your name *and* your number when you answer the phone; it just may be a nuisance caller trying numbers at random, who will then know who to ask for if he rings again. If the caller asks what your number is, ask what number he wants, and then tell him whether he is right or wrong. It is quite often the case that a nuisance caller is someone who knows you. Perhaps it is a man who has built up some kind of fantasy around you. Or it could be somebody, male or female, who has a grudge against you, or one of your friends or family.

There are callers who set out to upset you by ringing at times calculated to disturb your sleep. They'll ring at midnight perhaps, and then several more times during the small hours. If this happens to you there is only one solution and that is to unplug the phone or turn the bell off when you go to bed. You can at least take some comfort from the fact that whoever is calling is losing his or her own sleep. For anything from £50 to £200 you could invest in an answering machine which will take the call for you.

What you can do

If you become really worried by someone pestering you on the phone and if there isn't a man in your house who can take over the job of answering the phone for a while, I would strongly recommend buying an answering machine. On the whole, the

An answering machine is a worthwhile investment if you're receiving unpleasant phone calls.

cheaper ones are as effective as the more expensive models, but it is useful to get one with a monitor so that you can pick up the phone and listen but not speak if it is someone you do want to talk to. If you live alone, you could ask a male friend to record the answering message for you. And it's a good idea to give the impression that there are several people living in the house.

Some of the more expensive machines have a facility for recording phone conversations, and if you are receiving threatening calls, you could try telling the caller that he is being recorded and that you will be giving the tape to the police. If the caller is very persistent British Telecom can intercept your calls for you and try to filter out the undesirable ones, although not all exchanges are equipped to do this. It also has the disadvantage of irritating people who are trying to phone you for perfectly legitimate reasons.

You can also ask British Telecom to change your number, as long as you are very careful who you give the new one to. And as a last resort you can ask to have all your incoming calls barred. This is very restricting of course, as you can then only use your phone for outgoing calls.

What the law says
Making threatening or obscene phone calls is a criminal offence under the 1984 Telecommunications Act, but in reality there is very little the police can do to find out who a nuisance caller is. Tracing calls is not as easy as it looks in some of the cops and robbers movies. It takes time, and British Telecom will only undertake to trace a call on specific instructions from the police in the course of a particular investigation. But you should report the calls anyway, and help the police by logging the time each call is received and exactly what is said.

If the police think you could be in any danger, they may detail a patrol car to pass your house at regular intervals, or they may suggest you stay with a friend for a while, but it is rare for anyone to be physically hurt by someone who has been making unpleasant phone calls. Both the police and British Telecom take the view that anyone who really intends to harm you is very unlikely to telephone you first.

If you need advice, British Telecom publish a free leaflet called *Nuisance Calls*, and the customer service manager of your local telephone area can help you decide what further action you might take.

Callers at the door

Since we started the *Crimewatch* programme in 1985, I have become aware that it's plain common sense to check exactly who any caller is before you open your door – whether just to talk to them or to let them in. There is no need to be nervous or over-anxious, but just taking a few basic precautions should ensure that *you* will never be one of those people we feature so often on the programme who have fallen prey to the bogus 'telephone engineer' or 'Water Board official' or 'gas meter reader'. He only needs a few minutes in your home to make off with all the cash and valuables he can find. The victims of this type of conman are very often the elderly – people who were brought up before the days of cheque books and bank accounts – who would rather keep their savings in a teapot or under the mattress than trust strangers at a bank or post office to look after it for them. Thieves know this, and they know all the usual 'hiding places'. It seldom takes them long to find what they are after. I have already made a heartfelt plea for people not to keep large sums of money in the house, and to invest in a small safe if it really is unavoidable (see page 29).

Most callers will of course be quite genuine, but we have all read the stories of people handing over cash to a 'workman' who says he can mend their chimney, or repair the roof, or tarmac the drive – all at marvellous cut-price rates. Money is handed over for the 'purchase of materials', and neither the 'workman' nor the cash are ever seen again.

Then there is the 'antique dealer' who offers to buy your furniture for what sounds like a reasonable price but is really well below its true value. Once again, the victims of this type of con are mostly elderly people who are likely to undervalue the old furniture and 'knick-knacks' they've known since childhood. To them, new, modern things often seem much more valuable than their antique possessions.

We always talk about con*men*, but there are con-*women* too. In 1986 on *Crimewatch* we reported the case of two women who, posing as officials from the local social security department, had been persuading elderly people to part with their pension books on the grounds that they were needed for a routine check, and that the books would be returned very soon. Needless to say, the pension books were never seen again by their owners; and the women cashed the pensions at post offices all around the country. The DHSS reimbursed the pensioners, but they were all left in a state of shock and upset at what had happened to them. Since our programme, the women seem to have been lying low. Perhaps they are waiting to start their operation again when they think people have forgotten about them. So beware!

Children aren't always as innocent as they seem either. One common trick is for two children to knock on the door and tell you their ball has gone into your back garden. While you take one of them outside to look for it, the other one ransacks the place. Of course, you can thwart that one by asking them to wait, closing the door and getting the ball (if it exists!) yourself.

If someone calls for jumble for a worthy cause, check that they are legitimate and shut the door rather than leaving it ajar while you go upstairs to look for something. Most people are honest, but all the same I'm afraid it just isn't wise to be so trusting.

When selling their homes, women should certainly avoid showing people round the house when they are alone. Make sure there is a representative from the estate agent or a friend with you. Last year we reported on the case of a woman who was seriously assaulted by a man who would look out for 'For Sale' boards and pose as a prospective buyer asking to see round properties without first making an appointment through the estate agent. After the programme, police received reports of several similar incidents around the country. I would advise not displaying a 'For Sale' board at all. Leave the advertising up to the estate agent. Make them earn their commission!

For just a few pounds you can ensure that you get a good look at every caller and the chance to examine their credentials before they have any chance of stepping over the threshold. All you need is a spyhole door viewer and a good strong door chain or door limiter.

Door viewers

If your door is made of solid wood it is a simple matter to fit a spyhole, and there are two basic types. The first is a small lens which gives you a wide-angle view of the other side of the door. The second is a small two-way mirror set in the door – you can see through this type of spyhole and move it aside, in order to talk to the visitor, without having to open the door at all. The aperture is just big enough to push a note or the caller's identity papers through, and a strong metal cover closes the hole completely when it is not in use. A reasonable door viewer costs about £5. They can also be fitted in hollow doors but it's advisable to consult a locksmith.

Of course a door viewer is no use at night unless there is a light outside, so fit a porch light if you can. If you live in a block of flats where there is no light in the passageways (landlords often fit push-button timer switches which allow just enough time for someone to climb the stairs before the lights go off again), think about forming a Neighbourhood Watch scheme. With all the residents banded together plus the support of local police, you stand a good chance of persuading the freeholder to install proper lighting (see page 45 on Neighbourhood Watch schemes). In the meantime, always ask callers to press the timer switch so that you can see them via your door

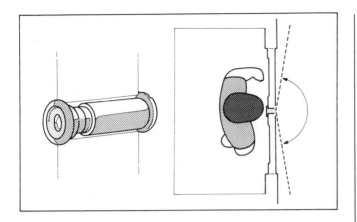

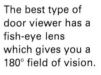

The best type of door viewer has a fish-eye lens which gives you a 180° field of vision.

viewer. If you can't see who's there, *don't* open the door!

Exterior lighting is a good deterrent to thieves anyway, as it means they cannot take their time to break in through doors or windows using the cover of darkness (see page 30 on security lighting).

Door chains and limiters

The most important point about having a door chain or a door limiter is to make sure you use it every time you have to open the door to talk to a visitor you do not recognise. As long as it is positioned properly, it should allow the door to open just enough for you to see identity papers, or to receive a letter or package, but not wide enough for anyone to be able to put a hand round the door to release the chain and push their way in. Choose the stoutest chain you can find. It should be strong enough to resist a fairly hefty kick to the door and will cost just under £4. Limiters have a sliding bar rather than a chain and are a little stronger than door chains. They should cost between £4 and £5.

NB: A note for disabled and elderly people – don't keep the chain on all the time in case there is an emergency and someone has to get in to help you.

In the chapter about locks, I said that it was no use buying the strongest and most expensive locks if you then fit them using weak screws. The same applies to chains and limiters. Use strong, best-quality screws – at least 30 millimetres long – and angle them into the woodwork in different directions so that the fitting cannot easily be wrenched out of the door jamb. In fact you can now buy proper security screws which are parallel-sided so that they grip along their entire length (see illustration).

Entryphone systems

Many flats and houses now have entryphone systems which allow you to speak to the caller before deciding whether to let him in by pressing the button to release the lock on the front door. A few words of warning from the police – although entryphones control *entry* to a block of flats, they do not ensure that the caller *leaves* the building. For this reason, you should only let in visitors for *your* flat, not for any of the other flats in the building. Make sure you know who they are, and treat your entryphone door as you would any other door. Of course, even with an entryphone, you should still use your door chain and spyhole – because you need to have a look at him and check his identity before letting him in. If the caller is a stranger, try to watch him (or her) off the premises from your window. And if you're suspicious, call the police.

There are also closed circuit security cameras which are often combined with entryphone systems so that you can see as well as hear the person you are talking to. These cost hundreds of pounds. Spyholes are a lot cheaper!

If in doubt, keep them out

Having taken all these precautions, the resounding advice from the police is 'IF IN DOUBT KEEP THEM OUT'. You do not have to let anyone into your home if you do not want to. Remember:

● If you are not sure about a caller, say you will telephone his company or organisation (and this includes the gas, telephone and electricity boards) to make an appointment at a time more convenient to you (and when you can arrange to have a friend with you if you like). Don't use the phone number on the card he gives you – it might be the number of an accomplice. Look it up in the telephone book or ask directory enquiries instead.

● Never let anyone into your home unless you are sure they are who they say they are. Don't be too embarrassed to examine their identity papers carefully. Genuine callers will understand.

● Don't leave a caller alone in a room unless you know they are genuine.

● If you do receive a visit from a suspicious stranger, let the police know about it straight away. It will alert them to look out for him and perhaps spare someone else from falling for his story. Try to give a good description of him (see page 43).

Rape and sexual assault

Rape is still, thankfully, one of the rarer crimes, but, once again, it is well worth confronting the possibility in your mind. If it did ever happen to you, the fact that you had thought things through could be of tremendous help and support. If you should ever become the victim of a rape or sexual assault, the first thing you will have to decide is whether or not to report it to the police. There are two reasons for going to the police: first, because you have the right to justice – to make sure whoever did it does not get away with it; and secondly for the good of other women, to try to catch him before he attacks again.

If you do decide to report the rape, there's no point in pretending that this won't be a further ordeal. It is important, first of all, that you contact the police station as soon as possible after the rape because the police will need to take note of your appearance and behaviour for corroborating evidence and any delay may go against you later in court.

You have the right to insist on there being a woman police officer present, and in most police forces now there are officers who have been specially trained in the sensitive business of taking statements from victims of rape. All the same, you must be prepared to face lengthy questioning which will not always seem sympathetic and will often be very personal.

You will probably have to describe what happened several times over, at a time when you may be too upset to talk to anyone except someone you love and trust. But it is important for the police to make sure they have all the details, and for this reason you will have to try to be as coherent and articulate as you can. This is why police advise you not to take alcoholic drink or tranquillisers before they interview you. Eventually you'll be asked to make a statement which will be written down and then given to you to read through. You can make any changes you feel are necessary before you sign it.

You will have to go through a medical examination, so it is important to resist the overwhelming temptation to have a bath, which would of course destroy vital forensic evidence.

The medical examination will have to be carried out by someone with the necessary forensic expertise. Many police surgeons now are women and you have the right to ask for a woman doctor if you prefer. This may help to avoid the feeling some women have that they are being violated all over again. You can also ask for your own GP to be present if you feel you would like that extra reassurance.

The police may want to take some or all of your clothes away for forensic examination, so take a warm change of clothing with you. Unless you are a very strong person, don't try to go through all this alone. Take someone with you to the police station for comfort and moral support.

Rape crisis centres
If you'd rather not involve anyone you know, then do contact your local Rape Crisis Centre who have more than 60 volunteer telephone counsellors in every major city in the United Kingdom available at all times of the day and night. I would advise speaking to them anyway, as soon as possible after the rape has happened, because they will be able to give you sensitive and precise advice on possible courses of action and help you decide which is best in your particular circumstances. They are trained to put your needs before all other considerations and can tell you what to expect from the police and indeed from friends, relatives, employers, neighbours and all the people around you. They know all about the legal and medical procedures you may have to go through, and can usually send someone with you to the police

station, to doctors, VD clinics, and to court if there is to be a prosecution.

Victims support schemes

The other organisation that can offer support and reassurance is the Victims Support Scheme if there is one in your area (see page 115). Like the Rape Crisis volunteers, they can go with you to police stations, doctors and courts. They are also trained to understand what you are likely to be going through, and to help you cope with the various emotions you will experience as you gradually come to terms with what has happened to you. The most common reactions are shock, fear, helplessness, guilt, shame and, above all, anger. Your loved ones won't always be able to understand or handle all this so they will need understanding too. This is why the Victims Support Scheme and the Rape Crisis Centre can be so invaluable. Both organisations can also advise you if you decide to apply to the Criminal Injuries Compensation Board for financial compensation as a result of rape or sexual assault.

Medical treatment

Whether or not you report the rape to the police, you *must* visit a doctor as soon as possible for tests to find out whether you have contracted any disease associated with sexual contact.

If you think there's any chance that you have become pregnant, you can ask your doctor to prescribe what is commonly known as the 'morning after pill' which, as long as it is taken within 48 hours of the rape, should bring on early menstrual bleeding and prevent implantation of a fertilised ovum. This pill does sometimes have unpleasant side effects but your doctor will advise you. You may prefer to risk waiting until you can take a pregnancy test.

Going to court

When the police have arrested and charged someone with the rape, the next ordeal for you will be the
trial. You have the right to anonymity during the pro-
ceedings. Right from the start, when you first report
the rape, you can ask for your name not to be used in
court. The law now protects women to some extent
against having their sexual history paraded in court,
but it is the job of the accused's counsel to try to
discredit your evidence in any way possible, which
can be extremely distressing. You will have to keep
reminding yourself why you reported what happened
in the first place, that you are there in court because
you are defending your rights and those of all women
to walk freely, where they like and when they like.
You are not to blame for what happened. It may also
help to remember that although you are a rape victim,
you are also a rape survivor.

Useful addresses

Rape Crisis Centre headquarters (can put you in
touch with your nearest centre), PO Box 69, London
WC1X 9NJ.
Tel: 01 837 1600 (24-hour line)
     01 278 3956 (office)

National Association of Victims Support Schemes
(can put you in touch with nearest local counsellor),
Cranmer House, 39 Brixton Road, London SW9 5DZ.
Tel: 01 735 9166

Women's Aid Federation (England), 374 Gray's Inn
Road, London WC1.
Tel: 01 837 9316

or

c/o Manchester Women's Centre, 116 Portland Street, Manchester.
Tel: 061 228 1069

Welsh Women's Aid, Incentive House, Adam Street, Cardiff, South Wales.
Tel: 0222 462291

Scottish Women's Aid, Ainslie House, 11 St Colme Street, Edinburgh.
Tel: 031 225 8011

Samaritans (Head Office), 17 Uxbridge Road, Slough, Berkshire SL1 1SN.
Tel: 0753 32713

Criminal Injuries Compensation Board, Whittington House, 19–30 Alfred Place, London WC1E 7EJ.

Keeping children safe

Child abduction and sexual abuse are subjects we would all rather not have to think about or talk about. Unfortunately, we can no longer afford to ignore the problems that children and young adults have to face in today's world. Being physically smaller and weaker, and with their limited experience of life, they are vulnerable to a whole range of dangers – from the driver who doesn't see the zebra crossing until it's too late, to the bully who tries to force them to hand over some prized possession, to the child molester lingering outside the playground hoping to accost an unsuspecting youngster.

It is our responsibility as adults, whether parents, teachers or friends, to make sure that we do prepare children for these dangers, not by turning them into frightened little mice, but by making them aware that these dangers exist and teaching them how they can avoid them.

In this section I have drawn on my own experience working with Esther Rantzen's 'ChildLine' and information kindly provided by various organisations, particularly Kidscape, who publish an excellent free leaflet for parents and children. It includes the Kidscape Code for children to read themselves which is written in simple language they can understand. Send an s.a.e. to:

Kidscape
82 Brook Street
London W1Y 1YG

Stranger danger
● Obviously children are most at risk from molesters or abductors when they are alone, so they must be made aware that it is dangerous to play in deserted places out of sight of other people, and that they should stick with a group of their friends rather than play out on their own.

● Most parents warn their children not to talk to strangers, but make sure very young children understand what you mean by the word 'stranger'. The trouble is, we try to teach our children to be polite, and if someone approaches them in the street and seems to be 'just being friendly', they may not want to seem rude. So we have to explain that in this situation, the usual rule must be disregarded. They should pretend not to hear the person and run or walk quickly away. Most well-meaning adults these days know enough not to approach a child alone unless that child is obviously in distress.

● Teach your kids that if a stranger should ever grab them or attack them in any way, again all the normal rules can and must be broken. Telling lies, kicking, scratching, biting, screaming and shouting – all are *good* things to do if it means keeping themselves from harm. Tell them to yell 'No' or 'Help, I don't know this person' and *run* towards any area where there are people about.

● Make sure they know that if a stranger ever tries to persuade them to get into a car, offering them sweets, or a lift home in the rain, or a visit to a fairground perhaps – that they should *never ever* accept, no matter how tempting the offer sounds or how nice the person seems. The stranger may even say that Mum or Dad sent him, so tell your child that you would never do that, and not to go anywhere with a stranger, ever, under any circumstances. Tell your children that if it should happen one day that you cannot collect them for some reason, that you will phone the head teacher to say who will be collecting them instead of you, so that the teacher can tell them in advance what to expect.

● The best thing for a child to do if he is being followed by a stranger is not to hide behind bushes or cars or in doorways, but to go where there are people

Tell your child that you'll always let them know in advance any change in your normal arrangements for meeting them from school. They should never go off with a stranger, no matter how plausible his or her story.

about, to a shop or a neighbour's house or, *as a last resort*, to ring the doorbell of any house where it looks as though people are at home.

● Every so often, ask your children to pretend that one of the situations I have described here has arisen and to tell you what they would do. Make a game out of it with a group of their friends or with their brothers and sisters. This will help to fix all your instructions in their minds and increase their confidence, rather than just make them feel too frightened to go anywhere without you.

How to get help
● Every child must know his or her full name, address and telephone number.

● Teach your children how to make a public telephone call either by direct dialling or through the operator by dialling 100. Make sure they know how to telephone their parents at home or at work and also a neighbour or another responsible person whom they know and trust.

● Tell them always to keep back enough money to

get home and never spend it on anything else. But teach them how to make a reverse charge call in case they do ever find themselves penniless and stranded.

● Teach them how to make an emergency phone call by dialling 999. Tell them exactly what happens – perhaps by turning it into a 'Let's pretend' game. The first thing the operator will say is 'Emergency: what service do you require. They should say 'Police'. The operator will then ask for their number – that means they must give the number they are calling from, which is usually printed on the telephone. The next voice they hear will be the police who will ask again what number they are speaking from. The police will want to know their name and where they are so that they can find them. Then they will ask what is wrong. This may sound as though it takes a long time but tell your children that usually it all happens very quickly. Make sure they understand, though, that they must only dial 999 if they are really in trouble.

● Tell them that if ever they should become lost or separated from you while you are shopping, they should not attempt to search for you but go to the nearest member of the shop's staff and ask 'Do you work here?' If the answer is 'Yes', they can tell him or her 'I'm lost, can you help me?' Tell your child *never* to leave the shop without you.

● If they ever become separated from you in the street, tell them to go into the nearest shop and approach a member of staff in the same way or, even better, if there is a uniformed police officer in sight they can, of course, always approach him or her for any help they may need.

● Children should not be left at home alone at all, but if this is absolutely unavoidable, warn them not to answer the door under any circumstances. Neither should they tell a stranger on the telephone that they

Teach your child never to leave a shop without you – and ask a shop assistant for help if lost.

are at home alone. Make sure they know how to dial you, a neighbour or the police in an emergency.

● Bullies can make life miserable for children and they often get hurt trying to protect a precious possession from a bully – usually an older or bigger child. Tell them to say 'No' without fighting, to try to enlist the help of friends, and to tell an adult. In cases of real physical danger children often have no choice but to surrender to the bully's demands. Tell them that, whatever happens, it is not worth getting hurt because, say, a bully is trying to take their bike and they are frightened that Mum or Dad will be furious with them if they come home without it. Tell them you care for their safety more than anything.

All these things should be said in a sensible matter-of-fact way. The important thing is not to fill the child with fear and foreboding.

What you as a parent should be aware of
● Know your children's friends, their names, addresses and phone numbers so that you can check

121

quickly on your children's whereabouts if you become worried.

● Take an interest in your children's activities, get involved with what they are doing so that you know what they care about and what's going on in their lives.

● Check that your children's school or day-care centre know never to release them to anyone but you or someone that you have personally notified them about.

● Don't buy your children clothes or jewellery with their names on them – it just gives a child molester the chance to win their confidence by pretending he knows them.

● Make sure they tell you where they are going when they go out, who they will be with and what time they will be back. Ask for a phone number where they will be. Explain that you have to know these things not because you are being the heavy-handed parent, but because you want to be sure of their safety. If they think you are being over-protective, tell them to indulge you!

Childminders and babysitters
Always check that your childminder is registered – either by contacting your local social services department, or by writing to: The National Childminding Association, 8 Masons Hill, Bromley, Kent BR2 9EY (Tel: 01 464 6164).

If you employ a babysitter while you are out, phone home during the evening to make sure he or she is actually there. If you use a babysitting circle, make sure the members are vetted in some way. They may not all be reliable, responsible people. Don't allow someone to babysit unless you know them or at least know something about them, their background and where they live; and make sure they don't ask someone you don't know to take their place at the last minute. It is also a good idea to ask your children, fairly casually, what they think of the babysitter before you use them again.

Sexual abuse

This is not an easy subject to tackle, but it's important to try to find an opportunity to approach the subject with your children, perhaps by telling them that if anyone should ever try to touch them in a way that they do not like, then it is quite right for them to say 'No' very firmly. Say that no one should ask them to keep a cuddle or a touch a secret, and that they should never have to kiss or cuddle someone if they don't want to. They don't always have to do what adults say just because they are adults. Tell them too, that you want to know if ever an adult (even one they know very well) does try to touch them or do something to their bodies that they don't like, so that you can stop it happening again.

It is most unusual for children to lie about sexual abuse. They quite simply do not have the experience or the vocabulary to draw on. For this reason, children who have suffered abuse may seem confused and misguided when they try to describe what has happened to them. If they start trying to tell you, or anybody else, what seems to be a strange mixed-up story, fight any initial instinct to dismiss it as fantasy.

The signs to watch for

Sometimes, perhaps because of fear or because they are too young to understand what has happened to them or why, a child will not try to express what has happened in words at all. Then, as the child's parent, only you are likely to notice the changes in his or her normal pattern of behaviour that will tell you if something is wrong.

123

These are some of the most common behaviour changes in cases of child abuse, although there could easily be other causes for most of them – so while it is important to be observant, try not to look for problems that may not be there:

● sudden fear of certain people, situations or places

● withdrawal, clinginess, fear of being separated from you

● excessive preoccupation with sexual matters and/or sudden intense interest in their genitals when they would normally be involved in their usual everyday activities

● re-enacting what has happened to their bodies using their dolls or cuddly toys, or perhaps trying to do the same thing to their friends

● eating problems – either loss of appetite, difficulties in swallowing, complete refusal to eat *or* a sudden obsession with food and eating to the point of becoming overweight

● sleeping problems – nightmares, fear of going to sleep, tiredness from restless sleep or bedwetting.

The *physical symptoms* of possible sexual abuse:

● pain or itching around the genital area

● bruising or injuries around the genital area

● vaginal discharge

● bloody underpants

● difficulties in walking or sitting.

No single sign is proof that there has been abuse, but if you notice several of these signs together, then be alert to the fact that something is amiss. A change in a child's behaviour nearly always has a reason. It may be that he or she is being picked on or bullied by other children in the neighbourhood or at school; perhaps the usual, familiar teacher is off sick or has left the class. However trivial a child's worries may seem to us as adults, the fear is only too real to them. Don't assume that he or she is just 'being difficult'. You can best help your child when you show that you have noticed that something is wrong and that you care and want to help him or her.

If your child is sexually abused . . .
Sometimes, despite all our best efforts in warning children about the bad things that can happen to them and how to stay safe, still the unthinkable does happen, and must be faced and coped with. Often the child will be reluctant to describe what has happened out of fear; fear of breaking up the family and home; fear of reprisals from the abuser; fear that somehow they are at fault; and fear that you, their mother or father, either won't believe them or won't love them any more. They desperately need your reassurance. Say you are glad they told you what happened. You can help them to stop blaming themselves by telling them that the offender has problems. Children are never to blame for sexual assault.

Being attacked makes anyone feel powerless. It is important to give the child back some sense of control by listening to their feelings and their account of what happened. Try and find out what the child wants and needs without communicating your own feelings of fear and alarm and anger. Otherwise you will only put more pressure on the child who will as a result feel more frightened, more confused and withdrawn, and even more unable to explain or understand what has happened.

Finding out that their child has been abused, the parents also go through considerable anguish. The first reaction is usually a mixture of shock, disbelief,

These organisations are on hand night and day to offer support to children and to their parents:

Childline Tel: 0800 1111 (free)

Kidscape Tel: 01 493 9845
82 Brook Street
London W1Y 1YG

Incest Crisis Line Tel: 01 422 5100
(Richard)
Tel: 01 890 4732
(Shirley)

Mothers of Abused Tel: 0965 31432
Children (Chris)

Organisation for Tel:
Parents Under (Linkline) 01 645 0505
Stress (Opus)

NCH Care Line Tel:
(National England – 01 514 1177
Children's Home) Scotland – 041 221 6722
Wales – 0222 29461

outrage, shame and a need for revenge. How you give vent to these feelings is crucial if you are to help your child cope with what has happened, and you will almost certainly need support and guidance.

The National Society for the Prevention of Cruelty to Children (NSPCC)

Head Office, London   Tel: 01 242 1626
For 24-hour referral advice Tel: 01 404 4447
(NSPCC London Communications Centre)
(See telephone directory for local branches in England, Wales and Northern Ireland.)

The Royal Scottish Society for the Prevention of Cruelty to Children

Head Office,
   Edinburgh   Tel: 031 337 8539

The Irish Society for the Prevention of Cruelty to Children

Head Office, Dublin   Tel:
                       Dublin 760423/4/5

The police and social services will investigate any case of suspected child abuse reported to them. And your doctor may be able to help with local contacts.

Index